THE
IMAGINE
PROJECT

FOREWORD BY DR. JERRY YAGER

DIANNE MARONEY

RN, MSN

THE
IMAGINE
PROJECT

Empowering Kids to Rise Above Drama, Trauma, and Stress

A How-to Guide for Parents, Teachers, and Counselors

Yampa Valley Publishing
5161 East Arapahoe Rd. St. 255
Littleton, Colorado 80122
www.theimagineproject.org

The Imagine Project: Empowering Kids to Rise Above Drama, Trauma, and Stress

The information contained in this book, although based on sound medical judgment, is not intended as a substitute for medical advice or attention. Please consult your doctor or health care provider for individual professional care.

Although every precaution has been taken to verify the accuracy of the information contained herein, the author and publisher assume no responsibility for any errors or omissions. No liability is assumed for damages that may result from the use of the information contained in this book.

Cover and Book Design by Andrea Costantine

Cover Photograph: Mackenzie Maroney

Please note that URLs are subject to change. If a URL is incorrect, please contact Dianne Maroney @ DianneMaroney@gmail.com

ISBN 978-0-9889951-1-6

Library of Congress Number 2017914680

First Edition 2018   Printed in the United States of America

10 9 8 7 6 5 4 3 2 1

1) Parenting 2) Education 3) Inspirational

To every child, parent, teacher, and human being—
may this book inspire you to keep going every single
day and continue to *Imagine* more in your life.

CONTENTS

ACKNOWLEDGMENTS

There are so many people to thank for helping me with the creation of *The Imagine Project, Inc.* and this book. My gratitude is endless; I honestly couldn't have done any of this alone.

To *Fred Perrin and Jef Burnard*, thank you for believing in my concept, having my back, and applying your amazing talent, love, and support to make it a reality. Our friendship means more to me than I can say.

My gratitude goes to all the wonderful teachers and counselors who took a chance on the project and supported its ever-evolving designs and concepts. I'm also grateful to those who have made the project a part of their classrooms and are making a positive difference in the lives of so many children. Thank you *Sam Alexander, Jari Chevalier, Diane Fern, Amy Ford, Katlin Jackson, Jan Lanning, Jordan Long, Lisa Mircetic, Melissa Orlando, Michelle Parker, Kristen Parsons, Kathryn Presnal, Mary Renton, Christine Robb, Brian Seppala, Marilyn Seymann, Luke Simington, Jessica Taylor, Bill Townsend, Erin Wassenaar, Lainee Wilmarth, and Lauren Zuiker.*

A special thank you to *Sam Alexander, Amy Ford, Jordan Long, and Michelle Parker*—you are very special and talented teachers—and incredible human beings. My love and admiration goes to each and every one of you. *Sam Alexander*—I truly couldn't have done this without you. Your help and support has been indispensable, all along the way.

I'm extremely grateful to the amazing editors that used their knowledge and wisdom to polish and make this book shine! Thank you to *Dr. Deborah L. Davis, Kris Jordan*, and *Helga Schier*.

Peter Hughes—You are a remarkable angel in my life, always guiding, loving, supporting, and helping me with work that is so powerful for kids (and adults). Namaste.

Thank you to *Dr. Michael Pierce, John Reed, Bill Shenkin, Dr. Josh Wallert, and Bill Young* for believing in the project and advising me on which steps to take toward a broader exposure across the country.

Thank you *Susan Hartley* for your love, support, wisdom, and amazing networking abilities! You are one of the most incredible human beings I know.

Thanks to *Justin Zuiker* for working so hard to connect me with the wonderful institution of Regis University. And *Marty McGovern* for connecting me with the amazing *Victoria Medina*. *Victoria*, you are a light in this world and will make an impact that will positively affect others. Thank you for your help with the project and book.

Melanie Smithson, your weekly love, tolerance, and support has strengthened and guided me more than you will ever know.

Jody Stevenson, Aazura, and Dr. Heather LaChance, my love and gratitude runs deep in my heart, soul, and spirit.

Debbie Davis, thank you for all of your help over the years and your wisdom within this book.

My deepest respect and gratitude to all those who supported my and my family's healing: *Aazura, Dr. Bakkar, Sue Boorn, Dr. Jianshu Cheng, Dr. Randy Jonas, Margaret Johnson, Dr. Heather LaChance, Dr. Jessica Riechert, Lauren Skye, Jody Stevenson, Steve Waldstein, Paul Wiebel,* and many, many more. I am standing, walking, and moving forward because of you.

To the readers, reviewers, and contributors who gave me your patience and wisdom: *Sam Alexander, Dr. Skylar Bakkar, Dr. Cheng, Dorreen Cumberland, Dr. Peyton Cunningham, Dr. Debbie Davis, Ava Diamond, Danelle DiGiosio, Dana Fern, Diane Fern, Amy Ford, Sandy Gardner, Barb Haines, Chris Keller, Dr. Heather LaChance, Kathy LeFevre, Jordan Long, Ges Lorraine, Michelle Parker, Ruth Nichols, Missy Norvelle, Cordelia Randall, Dr. Jessica Reichert, Patty Thompson, Andre Van Hall, Bob Wendover,* and *Paige Zahorik*.

Polly Letofsky, you rock!

Judith Briles, you have taught me so much.

Sharletta and Calvin Evans, you will forever inspire me.

Christie and Sydney Taylor, thank you for blessing me in my life and allowing a beautiful face to be on the cover!

Thanks *Judy Saylor* for believing in the project and our new-found friendship.

To all my amazing sisters, brothers, cousins, aunts, uncles, and friends, I couldn't have done this without your love and support—you are each one of a kind and all angels on this earth. My deepest gratitude goes to my kids *Frank, Michael,* and *Mackenzie.* I've made many mistakes over the years and yet in spite of it all, you've grown into remarkably loving, intelligent, talented, funny, passionate, and kind adults. Wow, how did I get so lucky? My heart is full because of you.

To my sweet, talented, kind, and courageous daughter, Mackenzie: This project began with your early birth, and you've been my teacher ever since. Thank you for being the best birthday present ever, and for your talent in creating the beautiful photo on the cover of this book. I love you.

Finally, and most importantly, to my unique, amazing, silly, kind, talented, loving, and supportive husband *Jimmy.* We've been through so much, yet we kept going and found a way to make it all work—and have a pretty remarkable life together! Thank you from the deepest part of my soul.

With Love and Gratitude,
–Dianne

Foreword

"One of the most difficult things for us to accept is there is no realm where there's only happiness and there's no suffering. That doesn't mean that we should despair. Suffering can be transformed."

—Thich Nhat Hanh

"**H**OPE" IS A TRANSFORMATIVE COPING strategy that allows us to direct at least part of our attention to the light at the end of the tunnel. Our imagination is what grants us this capacity to hope, as we envision our world the way we would like it to be.

But adversity and trauma rob us of this incredible capacity, and unfortunately, not all children show up to school with the same confidence, regulatory capacities, and hopeful expectation of the world and others. This book is about helping children and adolescents who endure high levels of internal distress to reclaim this capacity for hope that there will be a brighter future.

The stressors children today are struggling to manage are clearly articulated and compassionately communicated in this book. There is a growing body of research that shows that accumulated stress in childhood, such as abuse, neglect, exposure to violence, poverty, and loss can alter brain development and functioning. The physiological changes raise the risk of cognitive, psychological, and physical health problems.

Although negative experiences can have tremendous long-term impacts, positive experiences can also facilitate change and become a protective factor. For example, due to the research and writing of pioneers like Ed Tronick, Daniel Hill, Peter Fonagy, Dyorgy Gergely, Elliot Jurist, and Mary Target, we now understand the critical nature of caregiver responsiveness, from birth onward, which boosts the young child's developing ability to self-regulate. A sensitive caregiver reads the child's distress signals, makes meaning of them, and responds in a timely and effective manner. When the response is on the mark, the youngster moves back into a state of calm. It is through these consistently responsive, repeated, regulatory interactions that children develop the perception that life is often challenging but they can make it through with the combination of their own resources and the support of others. And because of mounting evidence that *how we use our minds can change the brain's architecture*, this serves as a powerful call to action for the use of effective interventions to help support health, growth, and restorations for our young people.

This book answers that call to action, showing how parents, teachers, and other helping adults can guide youth to face and overcome real and imagined challenges. And unlike many books that do such a great job identifying problems, this book fills the helper's tool kit with recommendations and tips. There is valuable information that might be helpful in choosing multiple interventions that can support the healing process for you and a struggling child in your care.

Dianne starts off with a grateful recognition for the important role that sensitive, responsive adults play in creating a safe place for young people to share their experiences, without either over- or under-reacting. She effectively communicates her understanding of how hard it is to hear young people's stories, and encourages us to trust that the very act of sharing and having someone present to hear them, see them and know them, is healing in of itself.

Her "Imagine Journal," is an intervention that capitalizes on our capacity for hope. It can help young people safely reflect on their experiences and envision a brighter future. It also supports the understanding that we are all the authors of our own life narratives. We often don't have a choice about the experiences we encounter in life. But we do have choice in assigning meaning to those experiences. And it promotes self-reflection, which is the ability to think and feel about thinking and feeling. This is important because *how we think* has great impact on *how we feel,* which impacts *how we act,* which in turn impacts *what we experience* in the world. The Imagine Project journaling process also offers both internal and external resources that can reinforce the potential for a young person's new imagined future.

As the pace of change continues to accelerate and the opportunities for all of us to bear witness to traumatic events around the world increases, there is an exponentially growing need for effective strategies in our homes, schools, and communities for supporting resilience in our children. We, as the elders of our society, must make important decisions about what types of experiences we want our children to be exposed to with enough repetition to equip them with the social and emotional skills they need to have to live in a global world. The problems we are facing and our children will face in the future, impact not just our families, our community, our country, but our entire planet. We cannot get overwhelmed by the challenges we will face. We must learn to *imagine* ourselves collectively, finding innovative, creative solutions. This book offers the reader many resources that can help our children transform their suffering and maximize their resiliency and well-being.

–*Dr. Jerry Yager*

INTRODUCTION

*T*he *Imagine Project™* began with an idea for my first book, *The Imagine Project: Stories of Courage, Hope, and Love* (Yampa Valley Publishing, 2013). In 2010, I began traveling across the United States meeting and interviewing ordinary people with extraordinary stories. In my two-and-a-half years on the road, I met so many truly remarkable people who had overcome incredibly challenging life circumstances. I asked each of these people to write their story using the word *Imagine*. It's a unique format, where every sentence begins with *Imagine*.... As I listened to and read these stories, I could sense that these people had acquired a deeper understanding of how much they had overcome and who they really were as human beings. And in follow-ups with them later, they expressed how writing their stories in this format encouraged them to believe in themselves and imagine new possibilities in their lives.

After the book was published, readers reported how much these stories inspired them to imagine new possibilities in their *own* lives. That's when I realized how powerful the *Imagine* writing process was. And I wondered: *Could it be used to help children?*

I've learned through my professional career and by raising three children, it is critical to help kids process and overcome stress and trauma as soon as possible. I've also experienced my own share of stress and trauma. Losing my mom to suicide when I was 15; having a raging, alcoholic father; and giving birth to an extremely premature daughter who weighed in at only 1 pound, 12 ounces—these experiences taught me how much our stories can define our lives—*and negatively*, if we allow it. What if there was a way to help kids who've suffered from stress and trauma? Could telling their stories in the *Imagine* format steer them away from despair and toward hope and healing?

So I talked to a friend who is an 8th grade science teacher in a suburb of Denver, to see if his students could write their own *Imagine* stories. The kids loved the process, and we were both surprised—and concerned—when we read them. Out of a class of 28 kids came deep, profound stories that offered a glimpse into the psyches of these children. Some children were dealing with what might be considered minor challenges like moving or fighting among siblings, while others were dealing with more serious issues like bullying or sick family members. Yet most concerning were the three kids who expressed suicidal thoughts. That day, I understood the profound value of this project.

I kept going—visiting classroom after classroom, listening to incredible stories told by children of all ages from all across the country with all sorts of backgrounds—wealthy to homeless; solid family life to broken homes. Here are five examples of *Imagine* statements from five different kids in five different schools.

A kindergartner: "*Imagine...wishing there was someone there to pick you up from school every day.*"

A 3rd grader: "*Imagine...being hungry—all the time.*"

A 5th grader: "*Imagine...being the shy girl in school and waiting every single day for someone to notice you—just once.*"

A 8th grader: "*Imagine...your parents always pushing you to be better and not seeing how good you already are.*"

An 11th grader: "*Imagine...the police coming to your door and arresting both of your parents for murder.*"

Every time I left a school, I knew I had to keep going. Children need a voice, a way to tell their stories. Their hearts and minds are full of challenging feelings, thoughts, and issues. The stories I heard were sometimes mind blowing and heartbreaking, but I quickly learned that kids are resilient, even when they are dealing with intense adversity. And I'm not just talking about at-risk kids, but all kids—even kids who have seemingly good lives with two parents who love them, a good education, a nice roof over their heads. Any child can experience stress—and they can be guided to manage that stress.

Some children experience brain-based, physiological challenges such as anxiety or depression, which can cause great suffering and even lead to thoughts of suicide. Many kids feel very alone and isolated in a social-media-based, high-paced world. It is common for children to worry about what the world is really like, about having to live up to high standards placed on them by their parents, about problems on the playground or with friends, about social media, and even about the stories on television or in movies. Then there are the kids who must deal with additional stressors such as poverty, hunger, homelessness, living in high crime areas, or challenging family scenarios, such as being raised by a single parent who is stretched beyond capacity, having little to no contact with an estranged or incarcerated parent, and/or witnessing violence. Coping with such challenges and stressors is incredibly difficult for anyone. Even with resources, it can still be very hard. Unfortunately, many children don't have sufficient resources to help them cope, which puts them at risk for destructive behaviors such as withdrawal, truancy, self-harm, aggression, delinquency, and addiction.

To offer children adequate support, we need adequate tools. Writing an *Imagine* story is a tool. And yet, while it can be a profound process, even life changing, it's not a stand-alone tool. The writer—child or adult—needs additional strategies and support to sustain emotional wellness on a daily basis. So while this book introduces *The Imagine Project*™ to a wider audience, equally important, it offers information to help parents, teachers, and counselors foster mental and emotional health in their children/students/clients. This book also takes a holistic approach, exploring strategies for healing and taking care of one's body, mind, and spirit, which are all critical to emotional wellness. By using the tools in this book you can be proactive in your home, classroom, therapy, or group.

This book also applies to you and your well-being. Chapter 9 focuses on taking care of you, the caretaker—an extremely important task! After all, you cannot nurture children without first nurturing yourself. You can only listen, validate, and believe in each child if you first listen to your own needs, validate your own worth, and believe in your own ability to succeed. And you certainly cannot invest the emotional and physical energy necessary without constantly and consistently refueling yourself. So another important goal of this book is to acknowledge your needs, promote your own personal and professional growth, and boost your feelings of competence and confidence.

And every parent, teacher, and counselor benefits from extra support/outside help. But it can be daunting to figure out where to go and what to do. Chapters 9 and 10 will help you decide where to begin and how to find more support. Read through them and see what appeals to you and trust your gut. Emotional wellness happens with daily presence and understanding of what is happening within your body, heart, and mind. The tools in the book will help you, and the children you love and support, move forward and seek contentment.

I have heard many parents say to me, "My child is a teenager or in college, the damage is already done. Will this still help?" The answer is, "YES!" I honestly believe because I have seen, heard, felt, witnessed, and lived it—there *isn't anything* that can't be undone and healed with a lot of love, the right resources, and some work. Please know that no matter the age, anyone can benefit from the tools in this book. It may take some time, but healing can and will happen.

A Note to Teachers

In any society, one of the most challenging jobs is education: to teach, facilitate, guide, and encourage the development of young minds. Education is often a thankless job, but it's also immensely important and rewarding too. In fact, without educators, citizens wouldn't be adequately equipped or inspired to carefully analyze social problems or seek compassionate solutions that work.

If you have chosen education as a career, your passion is key. But you also need to arm yourself with effective tools and strategies in order to implement your vision. And the more tools and strategies you have, the better equipped you are to not only offer a holistic education, but also tailor your approach to each child in your classroom. Indeed, whatever your pedagogy, children thrive with individualized teaching and nuanced encouragement that attends to their unique intellectual, emotional, social, and physical needs.

Throughout this book, you'll find "Tips for Teachers" sections that can help you apply the information and ideas into your classroom. In recognition of how busy you are, each section has bullet points for easy reference.

Emotional wellness is key to a successful life. Balanced mental health gives kids (and adults) the opportunity to succeed, no matter what their challenges and desires might be. Are you ready? Here we go!

PART ONE

Emotional Wellness, Stress, and Trauma

WHAT IS EMOTIONAL WELLNESS?

**IMAGINE
STORY
by Elena,
7th grade**

Imagine...all your friends' faces when you're saying
goodbye.
Imagine...the last look you give them.
Imagine...tears coming down your cheeks.
Imagine...feeling all alone when you turn your back.
Imagine...your last glimpse of what you called your
home for 10 years.
Imagine...wondering if these feelings will last forever.
Imagine...calling a new place home.
Imagine...everything being different.
Imagine...the pain you feel thinking of all the good
times at your old house.

Imagine...hearing it's ok, it's ok.

Imagine...someone reaching out and being there to comfort you.

Imagine...new friends.

Imagine...wondering if things are going to be ok.

Imagine...beginning to feel like yourself again.

Imagine...everyone laughing with you, not at you.

Imagine...having joy once more.

ELENA'S STORY IS COMMON. MANY FAMILIES move; some more than once. Between the drama, trauma, and stress of moving, Elena's *Imagine* story shows signs of emotional wellness. She's worried, expresses her feelings, processes her situation, and then makes the best of it by finding new friends and finding joy again. Life has many ups and downs, and within those challenges, a lot of drama, trauma, and stress can develop—more or less depending upon the age and personality of the child, as well as the nature of the event. Yet it's important to distinguish between "healthy coping" and "unhealthy coping" with whatever challenges a child is facing.

So before we talk about the challenges of stress and trauma in chapters 2 and 3, let's look at "emotional wellness," which promotes healthy coping. Emotional wellness is not a common idea or term that parents, teachers, or counselors talk about much, yet we sense how important it is to the health and welfare of our children. But what is it, exactly?

Emotional wellness is the ability
- to allow, embrace, express, and process emotions, positive or negative;
- to feel empathy and compassion for yourself and others;
- to maintain healthy relationships with family, friends, teachers, and others;
- to communicate opinions freely, but with kindness and understanding of others' opinions;
- to take responsibility for yourself, your body, your mind, and your actions;
- to know when it's time to have fun and time to work;
- to accept help when you need it;
- to have a healthy perspective on material "things";
- to bounce back after difficult life challenges;
- to laugh, feel joy, gratitude, and optimism.

Emotional wellness is key to being resilient in the face of any adversity. And since adversity is an integral part of life, we can't really shield our children from it. Instead, we can promote emotional wellness by giving them tools to cope—lasting tools that can equip them to weather all the storms they encounter throughout their lives. Here are some thoughts about emotional wellness and how you can promote it.

Expressing Emotion

From the time they are born, children express how they feel about what's happening to them and around them. As newborns, infants fuss or cry to tell their parents that they need something. During their first two years, they also begin smiling, laughing, verbalizing, and pointing to express their needs and emotions. Then comes the defiant word, "No!" This is often dreaded by adults, but it is an important milestone. It signals the child's growing independence and self-awareness, which are keys to healthy emotional expression. "No" is a child's way of asserting how they feel about what's happening. It's also a way to practice healthy boundaries and stand up for themselves, which are skills we'd all do well to master. For teenagers too, "No" is an important milestone revisited, as they prepare for adulthood and making their own way in the world.

And yet we adults can be challenged by these assertions. And many of us find it extremely difficult to deal with our children's expressions of painful emotions like sadness, disappointment, and frustration. Because of this, some children—especially teens—go inward and don't like talking about their feelings to adults. And yet, expressing emotion is extremely important. So how can we help children express their emotions?

Listen first, without trying to "fix" it. This is hard because it goes against our natural instinct to fix it by offering solutions, a different perspective, or evidence to the contrary. Instead, the support that truly helps is to simply say, "I'm so sorry. That must have been hard/sad/aggravating. *Tell me more.*" Then listen some more, which encourages them to go deeper into what happened and how they are feeling. Listening can be hard because it is painful to hear a child suffer. But if you can remain calm and simply "walk" *with* them, instead of *for* them, they can derive strength from your willingness to be a nonjudgmental witness to their pain and a patient, empathic companion.

I recently saw this strategy implemented by a mother in a grocery store with two girls, ages about 2 and 4. The 2-year-old was not happy—crying and trying hard to pitch a real fit right in the middle of the produce section. The mom took the two aside; she held the 2-year-old and didn't say much to her. She was simply a soothing presence, enabling her child to calm down and finally communicate what she was feeling. This mom was impressive—she was able to stay connected to the 2-year-old and did not get pulled into the chaos of the situation. She stayed calm and patient as she waited for the child's emotional reaction to pass.

Maintaining this calm is not an easy task, but you are more likely to succeed if you are diligent about your own self-care. Particularly if you practice self-compassion, accept your own emotions without judgment, and let them pass without blowing them out of proportion, you'll be able to extend this kind of compassion, acceptance, and listening to the children in your care. The benefit of remaining calm and listening is that it gives our children the opportunity to express their emotions constructively, rather than channeling them destructively. When children express themselves and we offer loving support by truly listening with compassion, we boost their self-awareness and confidence—and their emotional wellness.

Feeling Empathy and Compassion

Empathy is the ability to understand or to actually feel what someone else is feeling. Compassion is the ability to be a nonjudgmental witness to another's feelings without taking on those feelings yourself. Both skills enable us to respond with care. Reading the emotions of others, expressing concern, and showing care are critical to everyone's success in relationships, at school, with friends, and in our professional lives. Relating to others with empathy and compassion is also a hallmark of emotional wellness.

Children begin to develop empathy and compassion when they receive empathy and compassion from caregivers who validate emotions, offer comfort, and "hold space," which means quietly and calmly listening with care as a child expresses big emotions. Children also develop empathy and compassion by hearing their parents or teachers talk about other people's feelings, watching them hold space for others, and by following guidance on how to show concern. Empathetic, compassionate children might hug another child when they see the other child is sad, share a toy if they sense someone is feeling left out, or try to help when someone needs assistance. We can also teach empathy and compassion by giving suggestions. When I'm in a classroom and a student reads a powerful personal story, I often remind the other kids that this child may benefit from a bit of extra positive attention or a listening ear later on. This gentle guidance never fails—they always extend compassion to those they know are hurting. Children will rise to the occasion when they know when and how to show their concern.

Being compassionate with oneself is an important aspect of self-care. Change happens, challenge happens—accepting life's ups and downs and knowing we did the best we could is what helps us bounce back. Still, we are often hard on ourselves, thinking we should have done something different or better. Instead, by practicing self-compassion, we teach our kids the value of telling themselves that it's okay, that they did what they could. They might feel sad or mad, and that's okay, and maybe tomorrow they can pick themselves up and do something different or more. We can also model the perspectives of seeing mistakes as learning opportunities and accepting the twists and turns of our lives. We all hold great potential—finding our way through trial and error is perfectly normal and often, the *only* way we learn.

Maintaining Healthy Relationships

Emotional wellness relies on maintaining healthy relationships. We are social beings who benefit from interdependence, that is, feeling whole and competent as an individual and also able to connect meaningfully and rely on others for companionship and support. Keys to healthy relationships include knowing when to listen or when to speak what's on your mind or in your heart; when to stick around or walk away; when to hug or when to let someone be; when to help or when to let others find their own way. Infants first start learning about trust, sharing, and communication with responsive caregivers. As they grow, they also learn by watching the adults around them. Modeling appropriate relationship skills can be challenging, as learning how to cultivate healthy relationships is a life-long process. But by listening, modeling, and advising, you can help your kids build a foundation of skills that will serve them well as they dive deeper into relationships with friends and classmates.

Communicating with Trust, Kindness, and Respect

Appropriate communication is the key to successful relationships—and integral to boosting emotional wellness. Children learn to be kind by experiencing the kindness of others. Children learn to be respectful by being respected, such as when their feelings, ideas, preferences, bodies, and autonomy are valued by caregivers. Children learn to trust by being listened to. And children learn to be patient when they see our patience with them. Again, modeling these skills is key, and you benefit from the practice as well. Wait, breathe, listen, and respond—this is not always easy, but it is a gift to your kids—and yourself. Remember the words, "I'm sorry, tell me more." They are words of acknowledgement and caring, and show respect for your child's emotions and trust in their ability to bounce back from adversity.

Taking Responsibility

Taking responsibility for our actions promotes emotional wellness by allowing us to own up to our mistakes and, more importantly, to learn from them.

Everyone makes mistakes. When you see a child's mistakes as opportunities for learning important life lessons, you can encourage the child to take responsibility, make amends, and grow from failure, instead of shrinking and ducking in shame. Cultivating this sense of responsibility and growth also builds a sense of worth and control, which is the opposite of having to blame everyone else for what happened, or is happening, in order to maintain a sense of self-worth.

Balancing Play and Work

We live in a fast-paced world and we push for success, constantly expecting more from ourselves and others. But to cultivate emotional wellness, it's important to make time for work *and* time for play. Taking time every day to play or relax with your kids will show them the value of fun. All kids need a minimum of an hour a day to connect with their parents, either talking, playing, or relaxing. One of the biggest demonstrations of love is *time*, time spent having fun, just hanging out together, and feeling love. In chapter 7 you will read about the importance of play—physical play—especially outdoors. Balancing carefree fun with scheduled activities shows kids how important spontaneity, joy, and laughter are to their mental and physical health—and emotional wellness.

Accepting Help When Needed

Integral to emotional wellness is knowing when you need help, seeking it out, and receiving it with gratitude. Everyone experiences difficulty sometimes, and knowing when you need help and asking for it is courageous, regardless of what type of help it is— emotional, financial, educational, or just having assistance when putting something together. We often love to help others but struggle to receive. Show your children how grateful you feel when someone has helped you. They need to know you aren't perfect and you are willing to ask for help when you need it. Then they can more easily do the same.

Adopting a Healthy Perspective on Material "Things"

We all want to give kids a life better than the one we had. Many parents get into a habit of giving their kids "material things" as part of frequent trips to the store, on vacation, or as rewards for doing everyday chores. While this is fine to a degree, life doesn't really work that way as we move into adulthood. We often don't get to buy things whenever we desire them and if we do, we can get into financial trouble. Teaching kids that they don't always get what they want is imperative to cultivating delayed gratification, passing on your values, and modeling financial responsibility—all integral to emotional wellness. To help children adopt healthy attitudes toward money and material things, teach them the value of working hard and saving up for what's truly important to them, and model generosity and gratitude. When we are grateful for what we do have instead of demanding ever more, then "things" can be welcomed with joy and appreciation rather than expectation.

Cultivating Resilience

Life is challenging—some days more than others. Everyone has the ability to be resilient, but some kids are more resilient than others depending upon their genetic make-up and their environment. Two individuals with the same exact genetic makeup may have two entirely different expressions of their genes, purely because of environmental factors. Stress predicts 50% of how genes manifest. For example, in studies of identical twins adopted into different homes, researchers found many similarities (personality traits, interests, mannerisms), but also many differences, suggesting that environmental factors can "turn on" certain genes. Genes that make us susceptible to conditions like depression, cancer, and bipolar would "turn on" in one twin and not in the other, due to differing circumstances such as level of parental nurturing, the physical environment, school experiences, and family stress.

The way we respond to environmental stress also influences the manifestation of our genes. So even though we are influenced by our genetic makeup, coping can be learned, boosting our resilience. A child learns to cope with adversity by encountering difficulty and figuring out how to work through it. This process begins at a very young age—falling over when learning to walk, for example—and trials and errors continue throughout life. To strengthen coping, let your child struggle and make mistakes without jumping to fix it for them. Instead, let them do it. Research shows that sheltered kids have a difficult time being independent and learning to manage life as they move into high school, college, or the working world. Let them fall, listen with compassion, be a supportive presence, and whenever possible and advisable, let them figure out their own solutions. Your trust in their ability to prevail boosts resilience, a key feature of emotional wellness.

Cultivating Laughter, Joy, Gratitude, and Optimism

Watching a child laugh is probably the one universal visual that makes every human smile. I'm not sure there is anything better in life than seeing your kids laughing and enjoying themselves, particularly if you are involved! Emotional wellness means that your child is balanced—able to feel joy, laugh out loud, be grateful, and be optimistic. These positive emotions are integral to emotional wellness because they balance out the painful emotions that come with life's inevitable challenges. Positive emotions also let your child know that life is precious and well worth living. Chapter 6 talks more about cultivating gratitude and optimism.

A Note About the Sensitive Child

There are many highly sensitive children in the world ("Highly Sensitive Child" or HSC is an actual term used by mental health professionals). Research shows that about 15-20% of our population is highly sensitive. "Highly sensitive children" are more sensitive to their internal and external worlds. If you have a HSC, these descriptions will resonate with you. These children notice everything around them more deeply and they are often more easily affected by sensory stimulation, such as sounds, tastes, touch, smells, textures, movement, lighting, and facial expressions. Highly sensitive children are generally very intelligent and intuitive. They seem very wise for their age and often appear just plain different from other kids. The highly sensitive child can have a stronger tendency to become anxious and depressed in certain circumstances. Sometimes they are diagnosed with anything from Sensory Integration Disorder to Autism Spectrum Disorder. Elaine N. Aron's book, *The Highly Sensitive Child,* discusses behaviors, causes, and family dynamics, and gives great advice on how to raise a HSC. My oldest son and my daughter are highly sensitive—I wish I'd had Elaine's book when they were growing up!

If you have a sensitive child, even if you only suspect that he or she might be "different," you might benefit from reading more about the highly sensitive child. It can help to understand that they are more prone to reacting to stress and will struggle with processing trauma, and to offer them more patience and calm support. The suggestions in this book also apply and will help you provide effective guidance. As parents, teachers, and caregivers you will have to be more vigilant in making sure the HSC feels understood and is given the necessary tools to thrive in this often very complicated and highly stimulating world.

Everyday Parenting Tips for Supporting Your Child's Emotional Wellness

- Spend quality time with your children every day without any distractions.
- Ask your children about their day. "What was hard about your day and why? What was great and why? What are you grateful for in your day?"
- Praise your child's *effort* when doing things like helping around the house, working on homework, participating in sports, getting along with others—

versus praising only the end product. "I like how hard you worked/ how you persisted."

- If your child is resisting, acting out, or engaging in unwanted behaviors, before you react, take several slow, deep breaths to strengthen your ability to stay calm and then ask them what's upsetting them. This strategy helps you get to the root of the issue and address the real problem so you can determine a real solution for correcting the behavior. "Can you tell me what just happened?" or "Tell me about your day" can open up a productive conversation and can even boost a child's ability to self-correct.

- Ask your child "What do *you* need?" to accomplish what you are asking them to do. This question helps them to think about themselves and to understand their needs and personality better.

- Show them that you care about their feelings, their beliefs, their hopes and dreams—their identity. Avoid negative labels and judgments about who they are—for example, it's okay to be quiet, smart, funny, cautious, timid, sensitive, boisterous, athletic, artistic, or assertive. A child's personality may be different than you want or had hoped, but that's ok. It's good for your children to be true to themselves. See their strengths and their value, and validate them! You'll boost your success with this if you practice being nonjudgmental and true to your own self, embracing your own quirks, and honoring your own strengths and value to the world. Of course

there is always room for improvement, but know that you—and your child—are worthy, just the way you are!
- Teach them empathy and compassion. They will learn by watching you. Teaching them how to be compassionate, kind, and caring when someone is hurting or needy is important in the world today.

Tips for Teachers

Research has shown that social-emotional wellness in the classroom is critical to a student's success. In the February 2016 article in *Edutopia*, Weissberg et al. explain that social and emotional learning benefits students by helping them develop important emotional wellness skills, including managing themselves, understanding and relating to others, and making good choices. Developing these skills helps children maintain positive attitudes, have fewer conduct problems and risky behaviors, experience less emotional distress, and improve attendance and academic performance. (See also *Handbook of Social and Emotional Learning: Research and Practice*, by the same authors.) Here are some general tips to help you cultivate emotional wellness in your students:
- Welcome your students by using their preferred first names.
- Share a little bit about your life. They may trust you more if you show some of your personal side.
- Give students some say in the classroom set-up, minor schedule decisions such as time for stretching breaks, and decorations. These

decisions empower them, enable them to buy into the status quo, and promote a sense of belonging.

- Build a healthy classroom culture where students feel safe to take risks, fail, own their learning, and be problem solvers.
  - Create weekly small group "instant challenges" to promote group work, success, and opportunities to stretch and fail safely.
  - Teach dialogue structures that allow for feedback and fret from their peers, not criticism. For example: "When you did ____, it resulted in ____" or "I respectfully disagree with the idea that ____ because ____."
- Instead of the big teacher desk, change to a smaller desk off to the side. This gives the message that this is "our" classroom, not "mine."
- Foster an environment where expressing various emotions is safe.
  - Talk to your students about emotions. Model facial expressions; using visuals can be especially helpful for younger children and students learning English.
  - Explain that we all feel different emotions at different times in our lives.
  - Explain how emotions might show up in the body. For example, if you are anxious, your heart rate might speed up or you might have sweaty palms. Or being sad might feel like heaviness, a lump in the throat, or being very tired.
  - Use *My Imagine Journal* to help them express their emotions.

- Validate and talk to your students about how to manage their emotions, explaining that it's ok to come to you for extra support if they are troubled, such as feeling sad, angry, or worried.
- Set aside areas of the room that children can use to soothe various emotions, for example, a quiet place to rest and gather themselves, or a fidget area for children who benefit from movement.
- Offer frequent breaks throughout the day, to help kids pace themselves, give their brains respite, and balance work with play.
- Create a behavior management plan that is based on positive reinforcement rather than punishment—visit www.PBISworld.com for more ideas and suggestions.

2

HOW STRESSED ARE OUR CHILDREN?

IMAGINE STORY
by Kate,
5th grade

Imagine...being friends with a girl one moment and being bullied the next.

Imagine...not knowing what you did.

Imagine...feeling sad and upset.

Imagine...not telling your mom, feeling afraid she might be angry.

Imagine...your mom being comforting, not angry, when she finds out.

Imagine...telling your teacher.

Imagine...things getting better.

Imagine...getting more friends and loving school again.

Imagine...feeling angry and sorry for the bully.

Imagine...letting go.
Imagine...being free.
Imagine...being you.

~◯

STRESS—IT'S ALMOST A FOUR-LETTER WORD. AS adults, we often feel overwhelmed by living in a fast-paced, high-demand, amazing-technology world. Caught up in our own challenging day-to-day lives, we often assume our children live a relatively carefree life without stress. But children's lives can actually contain multiple sources of stress, including the pressures of peer groups, sibling rivalry, highly demanding schedules, and family expectations. It's also not unusual for kids to experience problems dealing with boyfriends/girlfriends, having too much screen time, and of course, handling social media. Tension and anxiety can often arise from within their own minds too. As children grow, they frequently feel pressure from their own thoughts as they attempt to understand who they are, how the world works, and how they fit into it.

Many children also experience stressors that go above and beyond what's considered typical and normal. Family life can be extremely stressful, such as when there is marital discord, mental instability, financial worries, abuse, or neglect. If kids hear parents, friends, or family members talk about troubling personal situations or community violence, this can add to their worries. Inappropriate exposure to media reports on crime, war, terrorism, tragedy, or political strife can also heighten a child's stress levels. And for some children, school is a source of excessive stress. Children may feel overwhelmed when they don't understand or can't deal with their workloads. Children can also be stressed by feeling socially or academically inadequate, like they don't fit in, or are not accepted for their strengths and weaknesses. Being bullied or shunned is extremely stressful.

In fact, research done by Stress in America™ on behalf of the American Psychological Association (APA) showed that teens, ages 13 to 17, tend to feel levels of stress similar to that of adults. On a scale of 1 to 10, teens reported, on average, a stress level of 5.8 during the school year (healthy is considered 3.9), and even in the summertime, a level of 4.6! Teens who face poverty, community violence, a challenging home life, and social deprivation (lacking close, in-person, one-on-one friendships) are at a higher risk for stress. Research also reveals that childhood stress correlates with a greater risk for adult illness due to chronically high cortisol levels. Most sobering, from 1950 to 1990, the suicide rate for adolescents, ages 15 to 19, has *increased by 300%*. In fact, suicide is the second leading cause of death for kids and adolescents ages 12 to 24. I hear from many kids that they wish they weren't so stressed but they don't know what to do about it.

Stress has not only an emotional impact, but also a physical one. That's because the core brain, which includes the limbic system, is constantly scanning the surroundings and making the nervous system in the body respond accordingly. For instance, when everything is okay, the limbic system secretes hormones that keep the body calm and productive. But when the brain perceives a threat— anything from seeing a snake to hearing a loud crash, from missing the bus to bearing someone's anger or criticism, the limbic system releases stress hormones (such as cortisol and adrenaline) into the bloodstream. These hormones increase the heart rate, mobilize energy in the body, and trigger us into survival mode: either fight (defend or strike back), flee (get away), or freeze (be quiet and still). Normally, after the threat has passed, calm can be restored to the body in less than 2 minutes. And as an adult, you can enlist a higher part of the brain to handle the stress and return to calm more easily, for instance, by soothing yourself with reassuring thoughts. This higher part of the brain is called the prefrontal cortex (PFC). The PFC is critical to emotional wellness as it regulates emotion, thought, and behavior. It develops slowly throughout childhood and into adulthood—that's why babies, children, and teens, whose brains are less developed, are prone to meltdowns when overwhelmed as they are less able to handle stress and return to calm. And that's why kids benefit from having caregivers who can help them by holding space for big feelings and offering comfort and reassurance during or right after stressful experiences. This kind of support, as well as generally not experiencing too much stress, also benefits a kid's growing brain, as a calm brain can develop a healthy, active prefrontal cortex.

Stress is a normal, unavoidable part of life. It's even good for a child to experience small amounts of manageable stress, such as frustration with learning a new skill, dealing with being late to a birthday party due to traffic, or worrying about saying the wrong line in a school play. Unfortunately, when a child experiences frequent, chronic, or overwhelming stress, survival mode becomes the norm instead of an occasional occurrence, and the brain and body stay in a stressed state. These chronic stress patterns can hamper healthy brain development, leading to an imbalance where the limbic system becomes overdeveloped and hyper-reactive, and the PFC remains underdeveloped. This brain imbalance can create significant mental and emotional issues such as agitation, anxiety, impulsiveness, hyperactivity, an inability to focus, lacking empathy, low emotional control, poor decision-making, and weak problem-solving abilities. Chronic stress can also cause a host of minor, and sometimes significant, physical health problems, such as an impaired immune system, slowed growth, aches and pains, and poor digestion.

How can you tell if a child is over-stressed? Look for physical and behavioral symptoms. Physical problems might include stomachaches, frequent headaches, acne, dizziness, bowel problems, bedwetting, change in appetite or food cravings, and frequent or lengthy illnesses. Behavioral symptoms of stress are varied as well: a child might become clingy; the quality of his or her school work might change; new compulsive habits such as hair twirling, nose picking, hand washing, or thumb sucking might develop; sleep patterns might change (too much or too little); mood swings might increase; a child might begin to lie or become quiet or secretive; eating habits might change. If there is any notable regression or worrisome change in a child's behavior and/or decline in physical health, it is important to step back and consider whether too much stress is the root cause.

How Can You Help a Stressed Child?

- First and foremost, spend extra time listening. Your careful, quiet listening helps a child feel heard and validated.
- Hold space for big emotions. This means being a compassionate, nonjudgmental witness while a child expresses him- or herself. Encourage the child to verbalize feelings, draw them, and/or move his/her body.
- Set limits, such as, "When you're angry, don't touch anyone or anything." Or, "Would it help to run up and down the hall for a few minutes?"
- Instead of interjecting interpretation or drawing your own conclusions, support the child's developing ability to analyze and solve problems by reflecting what you've heard and asking exploratory questions.
- Remember, questions that only require a "yes" or "no" answer can stop conversations in their tracks. And "Why" questions can feel pointed or punitive instead of caring.
- Ask open-ended questions that inspire sharing and reflection, such as, "How are you feeling?" or "What was your day like today?" Or simply invite them to "Tell me more."
- Reflect back what you heard, such as, "It sounds like you had a very frustrating time and got hurt by your friends today."

- Notice how your child is feeling and reflect on the emotions expressed, "It sounds/looks like you're really angry (sad, hurt, worried, etc.)."
- Ask for thoughts about why that happened and ideas for possible solutions. Let them know you can offer help if they want it.

Your listening and caring reflection can encourage children to move through stress reactions and painful emotions, maybe not immediately, but much more quickly than if they don't feel heard and cared for. By listening to them, asking them what they need, what they want to happen, what they see as solutions, and whether they want your help, you are also providing a supportive connection, teaching children how to manage stress, *and* promoting healthy brain development.

Still, careful listening and making time for reflection can be hard for parents sometimes, especially if you are busy or rushed. Tending every day to your own self care is also key, so that you have adequate energy to support kids through challenging times. It can also help to remember that taking the time now can reap long-term rewards. By consistently encouraging healthy habits and cultivating a strong prefrontal cortex, you are guiding a child along a path of emotional wellness, success, and contentment. This is a gift that lasts a lifetime. In the moment, try taking a few deep breaths yourself, feel the ground beneath your feet, and stay connected to your heart so you can be present and compassionately listen and support.

Sometimes all a child needs is a hug, your compassionate eyes, and/or a verbal acknowledgement that he/she is experiencing a stressful moment or challenging times. And when stress becomes chronic, overwhelming, or out of control, you may want to employ stronger measures. Refer to Parts Two and Three of this book, which offer specific tools for helping children handle stress.

Questions to Consider
- What has been happening in my child's life that might be causing stress?
- How does my child handle stress?
- How do I handle stress?
- What can I do to decrease my stress?
- How can I decrease my child's stress?

Create a Plan
Below is an example of a plan for helping a child deal with stress. You can tailor a plan to fit your child. Commit yourself to putting your plan on a piece of paper and place it where you will see it often. This will help you stick with it. You could put reminders on your phone, or use small stickers or pieces of paper in different areas of your house or car to help you remember.
- I will talk to my kids every day at opportune times, perhaps while in the car, during dinner, or before bed, asking them open-ended questions such as How...?, Was...? What...? or Tell me more. This will give them a chance to talk about what's on their minds, and give me a chance to listen,

support, and guide. To encourage sharing, I will keep an open, curious, compassionate heart.

- I will ask questions that encourage reflection.
- Examples: How was school today? How did you feel while spending time with your friends? Was there a point in your day when you felt confused, sad, or mad? Was there any time today when you felt proud? When did you feel happy? What was the best part of your day? What was the hardest part of your day? What do you feel grateful for? What else do you want to tell me about your day?
- I will ask questions that encourage problem solving.
- Examples: What do you think the real problem is? Did you try talking to him/her? What did you try first? What do you wish had happened instead? What other strategies do you think might work? How do you think others have tried to solve this problem? What will you try next time?
- I will weave downtime into every day, where we can relax, laugh, and have fun to offset or relieve stress.
- I will spend some time outside with my kids every week —going for a walk, drawing with sidewalk chalk, throwing the ball or just looking at the clouds or stars. This is one-on-one time, when I am focusing only on him/her.
- We will sit down and write our *Imagine* stories together or draw about what's happening in our lives (see chapter 5).

- I will talk to my kids about stress, how common is it, the best way for me to handle stress, and some ways they might handle stress.
- I will talk to my kids about responsibility, good judgment, and self-control even in difficult situations.
- We will create a gratitude journal/box together and play The Gratitude Game often (see chapter 6).
- We will set our intentions daily, and for important events in life (see chapter 6).
- Together we will practice random acts of kindness.
- We will have a family night every week, where we do what we enjoy together, such as play games, cook, garden, go for walks, sing, dance.
- I will give them lots of positive attention for the good effort they are putting forth each day, and also lots of just plain positive attention for being themselves. (A hug, a loving gesture, and an "*I love you!*" can be immensely affirming to a child.)

Tips for Teachers

Stress in a child's life away from school can easily transfer to the classroom, such as being hungry and not having enough sleep. Stress can also be created in the classroom, for instance, when a student is worried about assignments or dealing with social stress. Students who feel pressured might show stress by acting out, being spacey or inattentive, becoming needy or more emotional, engaging in disruptive behaviors such as interrupting or moving around a lot. In addition to the classroom tips in chapter 1 that promote emotional wellness, and here are more ideas to help students manage stress:

- Decrease extra noise and visual stimulation, keeping the room as quiet and uncluttered as possible.
- When possible, use daylight or full-spectrum lighting, rather than convention lighting. Harvest natural light by keeping windows free of obstruction.
- Give an adequate amount of time for transitions, as hurrying students can be stressful for them.
- Play soft music in the classroom.
- Use a chime or a soothing bell sound to get their attention or when they are moving to new stations.
- Give opportunities to write about their stress (using *The Imagine Project™* is perfect!).
- Take laughter breaks, such as sharing jokes, watching funny videos, or reading a funny story.
- Take movement breaks, such as dancing, yoga, stretching, or jumping jacks.
- Teach appreciation through talking about daily gratitude in a morning meeting and/or a wrap-up circle at the end of the day.
- Use mindfulness techniques like those suggested in chapter 6.
- When the teacher is quiet and calm, the class will likely follow!

3

CHILDREN EXPERIENCE TRAUMA TOO

IMAGINE STORY
by Kamia, age 18

Imagine...waking yourself up before the sun to take an hour-and-a-half-long bus ride to school.

Imagine...your legs burning from standing at a bus stop for hours to get home during a fierce Colorado snowstorm.

Imagine...having gone to eleven schools by the time you've entered the 9th grade.

Imagine...moving so often that you're numb to the feeling of packing everything you own in trash bags.

Imagine...knowing the term "at-risk" at such a young age that you didn't yet know the definition of "success."

Imagine...falling asleep much too early at a friend's sleepover because it's the first time in a long time that you slept in a bed—not on the floor.

Imagine...a single mother and her three children being crammed into basements, churches, and motel rooms.

Imagine...her abandoning you at 14 years old.

Imagine...finding out four years later that she, along with your older brother, were diagnosed with schizophrenia.

Imagine...never having a stable home.

Imagine...knowing complete and absolute loneliness.

Imagine...despite your loneliness, a silver lining of hope steadily vibrating in your soul.

Imagine...looking beyond the brokenness of your life.

Imagine...God bestowing you the gift of alchemy— turning pain into determination.

Imagine...wanting to succeed with the same intensity as you'd want to inhale while suffocating.

Imagine...yourself hovering.

Imagine...floating above your city during a sunrise in an unlikely helicopter ride.

Imagine...being blessed with such a helicopter ride that it inspires you to continuously remain thousands of feet above civilization.

Imagine...pushing yourself to succeed further than most are willing to go.

Imagine...making the decision to become an airline pilot, despite knowing that black female pilots who come where you come from are far rarer than being struck by lightning—twice.

Imagine…just like lightning, you are an immovable force.

Imagine…receiving your first pilot's license only two months after you became a first-generation high school graduate.

Imagine…finishing your first year in college as the first person in your entire family.

Imagine…fighting a constant uphill battle, but beginning to feel the warmth of leaving the shaded side of the hill.

Imagine…touching the clouds.

Imagine…sunlight breaking through those clouds with an iridescent beam.

Imagine…breaking through the circumstances you were given and getting a college scholarship to become a pilot.

~◌~

DO CHILDREN EXPERIENCE TRAUMA? ARE THE effects long-lasting? The answer to both of these questions is a resounding "Yes."

Unfortunately, trauma is more prevalent than you think. In a ground-breaking research project called The Adverse Childhood Experiences Study (ACES), Kaiser Permanente and the Center of Disease Control and Prevention studied over 17,000 adults in the San Diego, CA area. Participants were given a questionnaire asking if they had experienced any difficult events during childhood, such as a death in the family, physical or sexual abuse, neglect, parent imprisonment, or similarly traumatic events. Surprisingly, this study found that over 50% had experienced at least one traumatic event before the age of 17; 50% is a big number! It's important to note that the study was conducted on primarily white, middle-class, educated people, who are generally assumed to have had relatively easy, stress-free childhoods. As for children who grow up in urban poverty, the incidence of trauma is even more prevalent, with research studies documenting rates of 70–100%.

And unfortunately, trauma can have long-term effects. The ACES study found that high levels of childhood stress have been linked to emotional, behavioral, and physical ailments later in life, including depression, anxiety, violent or anti-social behavior, high blood pressure, heart disease, obesity, and diabetes, depression, arthritis, cancer and/or lung disease as an adult. The odds of binge drinking, smoking, and physical and mental distress are also increased. The more traumatic experiences, the greater the risk. This research has been validated repeatedly, yet most doctors and many therapists aren't aware of the correlation. Acknowledging and treating trauma, especially in children, can deter life changing adult health problems.

What is Trauma?

Experiencing "trauma" means facing a circumstance that overwhelms your coping mechanisms. We typically think of trauma as something more severe, such as an assault, molestation, or natural disasters. But any experience can be traumatic when it triggers a stress response and is difficult for the child to understand, process, or cope with. In fact, a wide variety of experiences can overwhelm a child's coping mechanisms, particularly when they are very young, experience too much stress in general, or have limited coping skills. Just some examples of trauma include experiencing a car accident, a bicycle fall, bullying, humiliation, being left alone, a dog bite, a medical procedure, loud arguments—the list goes on. Children can experience trauma even just witnessing a traumatic event—this is referred to as *vicarious* or *secondary trauma*.

We also tend to think of trauma as a single event. However, for some children, trauma can be recurring, such as being bullied day after day, witnessing frequent intense arguments, experiencing abuse in the home, or seeing repeated violence in the neighborhood or even in the media or online. Any continuous or repeated trauma is extremely challenging for anyone, particularly children.

Even incidents that happened before, during, or after birth—a C-section or forceps delivery, preterm birth, needing intensive care, or experiencing any health- or life-threatening complication can be traumatic for infants. Even though a person might not be able to remember or recall a traumatic event that happened in infancy, without the ability to completely process the trauma when it happened, the body remembers the sensations, and somehow, someway, some day in the future, that trauma may be revisited or get in the way. Therefore, it's imperative that we support them around processing and coping with traumatic life experiences—past or present.

For example, if a child is in a minor car accident and the driver of the car (typically mom or dad) is preoccupied with his or her own experience or with dealing with the other driver, the insurance, or police, the child may not receive adequate support to completely cope with the experience. The same goes for any other traumatic experience, even as seemingly inconsequential as a dog barking aggressively at close range. Fears or other emotions from the experience may stick with the child for years until they can be properly processed and let go. And unfortunately what is pushed down and not processed may come out sideways later as behavior problems, physical illnesses, emotional difficulties, or other issues. Here are two examples of what might be considered minor trauma rearing up and getting in the way of a child's growth or goals.

Nick was a 9th grade shotput/discus thrower just beginning to learn his sport. There are specific steps to the discus throw and the coach was working hard with Nick to help him perfect the steps needed before throwing the discus. Nick was a talented athlete, but for some reason he couldn't make his feet do these special steps. Of course, Nick was frustrated, so one day he came to me for help. I'm always curious about kids' past traumas, so I often ask, "What's the worst thing you've been through in your life?" Nick had a fairly easy life; he hadn't experienced any moves or lost a pet. His parents were happily married, his grandparents were all still alive, he lived in a middle-class, well-educated community. He had to think for a while and then he remembered a time when he was 8 years old. He was hanging out with his friends in front of his house. They were all having fun riding their skateboards. Nick hadn't learned to ride a skateboard yet, but he was trying. After a few attempts, he fell and all the kids laughed and made fun of him for being so "stupid" and "clumsy" (their words might have been even worse). Nick was humiliated. Yet, because he was a boy trying to be cool, he never told anyone about the incident, but his body remembered it. When I asked Nick if the steps to ride a skateboard were similar to the steps for the discus throw, his face froze, his eyes were wide open and he became emotional. He realized they were basically the same steps. As we continued to talk and work using Emotional Freedom Technique (EFT, see chapter 11) to release his traumatic memories from the earlier experience that were getting in his way, he relaxed, smiled, and got back to work learning the steps without any mental or emotional blocks.

~ ❧

Anna was a good student in 8th grade taking an average daily classroom load at a suburban middle school. In the middle of the semester, she began to get very anxious before and during tests at school. Her grades were falling. After we spoke for a while, talking about her life, Anna spontaneously began sobbing. She told me about the horse *she had lost six months earlier. She was very close to the horse, but her parents couldn't afford to keep it any longer and they had to sell it. Shortly after they sold it, the horse became ill and died. Anna had never been given the opportunity to express how she felt, sob, shake, and process the feelings evoked by losing her beloved horse. The anxiety she tucked away was showing up during other stressful events—such as testing at school. Thankfully, Anna was able to work through her grief and get back to being successful in school.*

These two examples show how unprocessed trauma remains held in the body. Later on, the trauma is revisited in the form of painful feelings that arise when similar emotions or actions are experienced during another stressful event or situation.

However, it's also important to remember that not every trauma causes issues. But, if a child is experiencing difficulty and you are unsure why, building a timeline of challenging or traumatic experiences can help you, as a parent, teacher, or clinician, determine which events are significantly affecting the child and focus treatment accordingly for maximum benefit. (See chapter 10 for more information on therapy.)

It's also important to note that a child's recovery from trauma may be impeded by a variety of factors, including poverty, racism, the severity of ongoing life stressors, family dysfunction, community stress, prior exposure to trauma, and emotional vulnerability. Such children are at higher risk of suffering from the emotional, behavioral, and physical ailments linked to high levels of childhood stress.

On a more hopeful note, many children are quite resilient and can recover from trauma without prolonged or severe disruption. Resilience and recovery can be enhanced by an adequate degree of emotional wellness and acquired stress-management skills, and when a child has family, cultural, or community support. There are many ideas and tools in this book for providing key support for processing and moving beyond trauma.

Signs and Symptoms of Trauma

Many of the signs and symptoms of trauma are similar to the body's stress reaction during the original experience.

Common Signs and Symptoms of Trauma by Age
Ages 0-2:
- Frequent fussiness
- Problems sleeping
- Poor eating
- Anger or aggressiveness
- Easily startled
- Anxious, fearful, avoidant
- Regressive behaviors

Preschool age:
- Irritability
- Poor eating
- Regressed behaviors
- Aggressive, excessive temper, acting out at home or socially

- Difficultly learning, memorizing, concentrating
- Imitating the traumatic event
- Feeling blame or guilt for the event
- Easily startled
- Difficulty making and keeping friends or trusting others
- Lack of self-confidence
- Problems sleeping; nightmares
- Frequent stomach aches or headaches
- Fear of being separated from parent

Elementary school age:
- Sleeping difficulties—too much or too little sleep
- Nightmares
- Eating problems (hoarding or avoiding food)
- Excessively angry, aggressive, or abusive towards others
- School problems
- Frequent headaches, stomach aches, or other physical ailments
- Poor self-confidence/self-esteem
- Feeling blame or guilt for the event
- Addiction or obsessiveness, such as with food, drugs, screen time.
- Sexual knowledge inappropriate for the child's age
- Unusual fears
- High level of anxiety
- Suicidal thoughts
- Withdrawal from social or family situations
- Difficulty trusting others
- Fear of being separated from parent/clinginess

Middle and high school:

- Sleeping difficulties—too much or too little sleep
- Nightmares
- Eating problems (hoarding or avoiding food)
- Excessively angry, aggressive, or abusive towards others
- School problems
- Frequent headaches, stomach aches or other physical problems
- Poor self-confidence/self-esteem
- Addiction or obsessiveness, such as with food, drugs, screen time.
- Sexual knowledge beyond the child's age
- Unusual fears
- Easily startled
- High level of anxiety
- Suicidal thoughts
- Withdrawal or alienation from social or family situations
- Difficulty trusting others
- Unhealthy or troubled romantic relationships
- Overly self-reliant
- Self-harm
- Feeling shame, blame, or guilt for the event
- Defiance
- Running away
- Starting fights
- Difficulty visualizing/dreaming about new possibilities in life

Questions to Consider for Yourself and Your Child

1. Have I ever experienced anything that might be considered traumatic in my life? Go to www.ncjfci.org to take the ACE test for trauma.

2. Do I still feel emotional when I think about that experience? Do I feel internal tremors when I think about that event? If either of these are true, you may need some help processing what happened.

3. Have any of my children experienced anything that might have traumatized them beginning with their prenatal and birth experience?

4. Do my children have any of the behaviors listed above?

5. What is the best plan to help my children if I suspect they have experienced trauma?

In my own life, I have experienced the negative effects of lacking the needed support and tools to deal with trauma. Barely 15 years old, I found my mom after she committed suicide. There weren't many resources to help me process and heal from that experience. For years, I felt very sad, ashamed, and deserted. I experienced an internal tremor whenever I talked about my mom, and sometimes I would even visibly shake. Thankfully, as I got older I found the proper help to heal. Now I participate in speaking engagements and tell my story with a sense of pride, knowing how far I've come. I see the same in many students as they write and share their Imagine stories—pride at having lived through, coped with, learned from, and healed from trauma.

If your child has experienced trauma, one of the primary goals is to make him or her feel safe— physically safe and emotionally safe— to express feelings. To address emotional security, earn their trust by acknowledging their emotions, offering soft and gentle touch, and saying "I'm so sorry" as you hold space for them, their experience, and big emotions. As always, remain a compassionate, nonjudgmental witness. To address physical security, create a special place that feels comfortable and calming, and non-stimulating (no TV, games, or other distractions), perhaps with comfy chairs, blankets, or pillows. This could be where they journal or draw. Decorate the area with accomplishments, positive memories, and pictures that represent what they like from their life or the world. Let them choose what makes them smile and comforts them.

It's also important to teach children (and adults) how to tune into their bodies, so they can know when they aren't feeling safe. When we feel scared, awkward, overwhelmed, anxious, harmful, uncertain, or self-destructive, we can feel sensations in our bodies, such as feelings of contraction, tension, discomfort, or feeling shaky or jittery, inside or out. These sensations are signs of stress hormones being triggered by the brain and launching us into survival mode and often accompanied by strong or escalating emotions. It's during these times we need tools to help us engage the prefrontal cortex so we can calm down and/or seek safe help. Tools include deep breathing, being held, going to a room where we feel safe, using tapping/EFT (see chapter 11), meditation, and getting adequate nutrition, exercise, and sleep.

The remainder of this book can help you support your child/student who has experienced trauma. It's important to note that grieving and processing trauma can take time. A child might make progress and then regress. Be patient and seek help when you need it—professional help can be particularly valuable. See Part Four or ask people you trust for referrals to practitioners who are skilled in working with children who've experienced trauma. By using the tools described in Parts Two and Three, you can help your children/students find healing as well as comfort in knowing you care.

Tips for Teachers

It's important for teachers to be sensitive to their students' trauma because a child who is dealing with the effects of difficult life circumstances (past or present) may have problems concentrating, high-level processing, decision making, language processing, sequencing information, and with memory (Terrasi, et al., 2017). These problems can arise because trauma can alter brain function. The brain becomes hypervigilant and easily triggered, and when a child's limbic system is releasing frequent or prolonged bursts of stress hormones, the child may be on constant alert, worried, anxious, or even shut down and literally unable to think straight. This impact can be minor or significant and can cause academic and social challenges at school.

Because trauma is so prevalent, it's safe to assume at least one (and probably more than one) student in your classroom is dealing with some level of trauma. It is likely that some students have experienced significant trauma in the past, and they may still be coping with the aftermath. It's also possible that one or more might have been traumatized just yesterday evening. Having an awareness of your students' past and current circumstances is crucial to supporting them and their success in your classroom. Whenever a student acts out, becomes depressed, shuts down, and/or has unusual behaviors, consider they may be dealing with a mild, moderate, or severe traumatic event that may have created short- or long-term issues for them. Here are some tips to help:

- Create a mindful classroom that feels safe, comfortable, and nurturing. For example, decrease clutter; arrange seating so that students can move around easily and not feel trapped; decorate the classroom with positive images and objects.
- Design a calming area in the classroom where students can go when they are feeling overwhelmed. (See www.calmclassroom.com and www.traumainformedcareproject.org for more information on trauma-informed schooling and classrooms.)
- Make referrals to your school's social worker, counselor, nurse, community liaison, and other allied school professionals to ensure that each student's basic needs are met, such as food, housing, medical care, clothing, and supplies, so they can be present and successful in your classroom.

- Create options from which students can choose, to help them feel empowered and in charge of themselves.
- Be patient, unreactive, and compassionate when a student acts out or shows unusual or big emotion. Staying calm and caring can help them calm down. Listening with caring eyes and reflecting back what they are saying or doing can help them realize what is happening. "I hear you saying..."
- Consider *why* a student may be behaving differently. Behaviors like being withdrawn, isolated or lonely, hyperactive, or uncooperative may be because something difficult happened recently (or in the past) and they need more help and support than they are currently getting.
- Learn your students' stories. *My Imagine Journal*™ is a good tool for this (see Part Two). Having your students write their stories can also help them process their tough experiences and emotions.
- Seek help from a school counselor or mental health provider to better understand how to help a specific student.
- Make modifications for a student when needed, such as longer times for testing, a safe place for them to sit with big feelings, or even creating an IEP or 504 plan.
- Keep a short calming audio/CD (with a headset) available for students if they are feeling emotional and need something to gather themselves. (Visit www.soundstrue.com)

- Read *Fostering Resilient Learners: Strategies for Creating a Trauma-Sensitive Classroom* by Kristin Souers and Pete Hall, and other materials on trauma-sensitive classrooms.
- Educate your administration and school district on the importance of trauma-sensitive teaching (Visit Traumasensitiveschools.org for more information).

PART TWO

Healing Through Writing

NOW THAT YOU'VE READ ABOUT HOW STRESS and trauma can adversely affect children, I'd like to share some tools that can promote emotional wellness and balanced brain development, which can help children manage stress and trauma, and deal with the challenges they meet.

The first tool is *expressive writing*, which can be easily implemented by using *My Imagine Journal*™. Chapter 4 explains the importance of expressive writing; chapter 5 explains how to help your children or students use *My Imagine Journal*.

Expressive writing is an important tool that can be used in conjunction with other tools, particularly those that nurture the body, mind, and spirit (see Part Three). By having a variety of tools at your disposal, you can holistically boost and sustain emotional wellness in your children or students, and you!

4

THE VALUE OF EXPRESSIVE WRITING

IMAGINE
STORY
by Joseph,
4th grade

Imagine...you left your country to have a better life.

Imagine...you need to travel by train so others don't see you.

Imagine...you need to walk in the desert for days and days.

Imagine...you need water but you don't have any for days.

Imagine...you are not with your family anymore.

Imagine...when you come to the U.S., you get a new life.

Imagine...now you can be with your dad, mom, and sister.

Imagine...having good grades in school.

Imagine...believing in yourself.

~ೋ

WHEN I GO INTO A CLASSROOM OR GET IN FRONT of large groups, I often ask, "How many of you like to write?" On average, about 50% will raise their hands. With children, the younger they are, the more they like to write; the older they are, the more groans I hear.

Unfortunately, many children are given negative ideas about their ability to write. Whether they are told that it needs to be perfect or perfectionism comes from within, they may struggle with vocabulary, grammar, and organizing their thoughts. Many kids are rarely given the chance to simply write from their hearts without worrying about spelling and punctuation. Yet, when they begin to write from a perspective of speaking their truth—a story, a challenge, or experience that is sitting in their hearts—something happens. At first it might feel emotional; thinking and writing about a painful event can be difficult to do. But once the flow begins, it can be freeing and empowering.

Expressive writing or journaling also has a healing quality, encouraging writers to process and find meaning from a difficult life circumstance, to let it go, and to create a new story for their lives. This kind of writing also allows the writers to feel seen, heard, and validated. And it feels empowering when they realize how far they've come and how resilient they truly are.

The Positive Effects of Expressive Writing

For over 30 years, researchers have been studying the effects of expressive writing. In most studies, participants are asked to take 15 to 30 minutes to write about an emotionally challenging, even traumatic incident in their lives. Typically, they are asked to do this once a day for three to five days. Even though the time spent writing can be emotional and make the writer feel vulnerable, the long-term benefits are positive. Research has found that expressive writing can

- improve grade point average,
- improve working memory,
- improve writing skills,
- decrease school dropout rates,
- enhance immune function (fewer illnesses and fewer trips to the doctor),
- decrease blood pressure,
- promote wound healing after surgery,
- decrease anxiety and depression,
- help people feel better about life, and
- lessen post-traumatic intrusion and avoidance symptoms.

Study measurements were done months, even years, after the writing exercises and positive results still existed. Pretty good stuff!

How and Why Does Expressive Writing Work?

James Pennebaker, PhD and Joshua Smyth, PhD can be considered the fathers of expressive writing. Their research has been foundational for understanding how and why expressive writing works. In their latest book, *Opening Up and Writing It Down* (Guilford Press, 2016), they explore the healing benefits of expressive writing. By writing down what happened (or is happening), we can organize our thoughts and verbalize the stress or trauma we've experienced, which allows us to confront, understand, make some sense of it, and gain perspective. We can even find meaning in difficult experiences through the written word, as putting our stories on paper can shed light on our problems and release the tension of keeping them in the dark. In contrast, holding in negative experiences and feelings merely creates more stress, anxiety, depression, or self-destructiveness.

We also have a basic need to express ourselves, speak our truth, and make sense of it, so we can move on. You can see this in the *Imagine* stories in this book. Kids and teens hold so much in their minds and hearts. When troubles are kept under cover, they remain unprocessed, take up too much space, and prevent kids from moving forward. Being "stuck" only perpetuates cycles of dysfunction, such as abuse, addiction, and poverty, generation after generation. Fortunately, expressive writing is an effective tool that can help kids process and let go of their stories so they aren't defined or limited by them. Expressive writing inspires them to imagine new possibilities, pursue their goals more effectively, and find a higher calling in their lives.

- It processes experiences by using language for expression.
- It helps clear thoughts and feelings.
- It gives insight into the event(s)— the how and why.
- It simplifies the experience.
- It brings meaning and closure.
- It boosts the ability to pursue goals.

Writing and The Therapeutic Healing Process

To promote a client's healing after a stressful or traumatic experience, a therapist will follow a process with three primary goals:

1. Allow the emotional expression of all feelings attached to the incident, felt then and now.
2. Help the client process the experience and understand what happened.
3. Support the client in rewriting their story, i.e., reframing the event so they can move forward and see new possibilities in their lives.

The beauty of expressive writing is that it facilitates all of these therapeutic steps toward healing, including imagining a new story. Expressive writing is not necessarily a stand-alone tool for treatment of trauma, but it can help facilitate the process of healing after mild or moderate stress and trauma. In cases of extreme trauma, consult with a skilled mental health practitioner whenever possible, in addition to using the expressive writing process. (See chapter 10 for more information on therapy and therapists; chapters 6, 7, and 8 for additional strategies that can promote healing.)

5

WRITING WITH *THE IMAGINE PROJECT*

**IMAGINE
STORY
by Easton K.,
5th grade**

Imagine...regularly going to some stranger's house and
hiding behind your grandpa every time.

Imagine...trying to talk to the stranger for the first
time but nothing comes out.

Imagine...still not knowing who she is but still going to
her house and playing with the toys there.

Imagine...not being as shy and coming out of the dark
to realize you have been hiding from your great
grandma.

Imagine...realizing she is the one who has been giving
you money and presents for the past 11 years.

Imagine...finding out she is going to assisted living and you being scared and not knowing what it means.

Imagine...going to her new home all the time and wheeling her around the building.

Imagine...one day waking up looking at your parents watching them cry and then realizing it was about that person you loved so much.

Imagine...going to her funeral and crying and thinking about all the fun times you had with her.

Imagine...putting the past in the past but having her in the back of your mind.

Imagine...thinking of her, which makes you want to strive and achieve.

Imagine...being better at things and knowing she wants you to work your tail off.

Imagine...knowing she is watching you, knowing she is not going through any more suffering, knowing she is in a safer place filled with streets of gold.

BECAUSE THERE IS SUCH A HIGH INCIDENCE OF childhood stress and trauma and so few resources available to so many, *The Imagine Project*™ and *My Imagine Journal*™ were created. The journal is a simple tool that can be used at home, in a classroom, or in any therapeutic setting, to help kids process difficult life experiences.

In classrooms all over the country, I have witnessed the transformation of kids and teens. At first, they walk into the room heavy with an experience—whether it happened yesterday or 10 years ago. After writing an Imagine story, they leave feeling hope and seeing new possibilities.

Robbie was in a 6th grade classroom in New Mexico, in a school for kids in transition, and he was homeless. He was an adorable boy with dimples on both checks, and an infectious smile. But he was hiding something behind that smile—something he'd never talked about before. Nine months earlier, he and his extended family had been enjoying a family picnic near a big river. His cousin went into the water even though he couldn't swim. The current pulled him under and he struggled to stay afloat. The father, Robbie's uncle, jumped in to save him, and while the cousin survived, sadly, Robbie's uncle, was swept away by the current and drowned.

Robbie wrote about the incident in an Imagine story. He even read it out loud to his classmates. I spoke with his principal a month later to check on him. His principal said that Robbie's mom had been asking to find help because Robbie had refused to talk about his uncle's death—until The Imagine Project. After writing his story, Robbie became his old, happy-go-lucky self again and his grades improved!

How Is *The Imagine Project* Implemented?

The Imagine Project is a simple expressive writing program that can help kids (and adults) process drama, trauma, and stress. As explained in the Introduction, this program evolved from the book, *The Imagine Project: Stories of Courage, Hope and Love* (Yampa Valley Publishing, 2013), featuring *Imagine* stories written by everyday people who have overcome incredible life circumstances. Many of them had reservations about writing their stories, but after doing so, most of them experienced a profound shift in perspective, feeling more positive and capable. The *Imagine* journaling process is simple enough that all ages can do it.

To implement *The Imagine Project,* use *My Imagine Journal,* which is a free resource. It contains a simple, seven-step process that successfully guides children to first think about, then write, and then complete their Imagine stories.

The *Journal* was created for parents, teachers, youth leaders, counselors, and/or anyone who would like to use *The Imagine Project* to help any child process drama, trauma, and stress. The *Journal* also teaches children about expressive writing, a life-long technique that can promote emotional wellness. Whatever the setting, the steps and techniques are basically the same.

Why *Imagine*?

Some kids are eager to write and even read their stories out loud. But for many kids, writing about something difficult can be hard because they may feel vulnerable and a bit like they are reliving a difficult experience.

This is where the word *Imagine* comes in. In *My Imagine Journal*™ every sentence begins with the word *Imagine*.... While using this format, writers can feel a safe enough distance from their own stories, so instead of feeling immersed in it, they become an observant witness to their difficult experiences. This enables the writers to feel protected rather than vulnerable, and while they may feel emotional, it's not incapacitating. Using the word *Imagine* also helps them express what's in their hearts and then visualize a sense of possibility within their stories.

When children's trauma is significant, it might be more challenging for them to write and they may need more support in the process. This chapter covers basic recommendations for guiding the journaling process for any child.

Getting Started

Setting. Any child or teen needs a quiet, comfortable place to write in solitude without interruption—either in their room, at the kitchen table, or at a desk at school (preferably without friends sitting all together). The most important question to ask about the writing environment is this: Do they feel safe? The safer they feel, the deeper they can go while writing about their emotions and experiences. Feeling safe can be influenced by factors that affect physical and emotional comfort. For example, do they have a comfortable place to sit and write, with lighting, temperature, even the pen and texture of the paper being comfortable or pleasing? Are they free from the intrusions of others, or the distractions of stimulating sights, sounds, or activities? Having a trusted adult present can help too, but some kids just want to be by themselves in order to focus and write.

Materials. Supply each child with a pen or pencil, something to draw with for the little ones, and an age-appropriate journal you can download and print for free, from www.theimagineproject.org. There are four journals, each one being appropriate for a specific age group: Kindergarten through 2nd grade; Grades 3-5; and Grades 6-12; and Adult. The Adult journal is for college students, parents, teachers, and anyone who would like to try it! If you can't download or print a journal, you can simply use a piece of paper and follow the seven steps below. There are lesson plans on the website as well.

Timing and Pacing. Writing an *Imagine* story can be fairly straightforward due to the seven-step process and simple format, but the writing speed will, of course, depend upon the age and skill of the writer. If you do it in one session, all seven steps can take a group of children about 60-90 minutes to complete. Some kids can do it in less; some may need more time. There isn't a time limit as part of the process, so if it takes longer, no worries.

Here's a rough breakdown of timing for the seven steps:

- Steps 1 and 2 take most kids 3 to 5 minutes each; some kids take longer.
- Step 3, the actual writing of the Imagine story, takes about 15 to 20 minutes on average.
- Steps 4-7 take about 5-10 minutes each, so allow 40 minutes for these final steps.

In a classroom setting you can spread the process over days or even weeks. The pace is up to you and how much time you have to spend on the project in a day. Any pace can be therapeutic. Younger children might take more time and take breaks, older kids may want to get it done or come back to it later—it varies with individuals, situations, and ages. In fact, expressive writing research recommends writing for 10 to 15 minutes for 3 to 4 consecutive days, but it is still helpful to do this project in one session if that is easier to manage. I would encourage you to support them through the first 3 processes in one setting if possible and come back to the last 4 if they need to take a break.

My Imagine Journal Instructions

The seven-step process guides the writers through considering different aspects of one's life, getting in touch with emotions, writing the *Imagine* story, seeing new possibilities, and setting goals. Below are the step-by-step instructions to give your children/students, followed by the reasoning behind each step and helpful hints for encouraging success.

Step 1: Celebrate. *What are three things you are proud of, want to celebrate, and/or love about your life? On the second half of the page, write down words that describe the emotions you feel when you think about these parts of your life.*

- It's always important to begin by writing about something positive so the writers realize there are good areas in their lives.

Step 2: Reflect. *Name at least one experience (more if needed) that has been challenging in your life, past or* *present. On the second half of the page, write down words that describe the emotions you feel when you think about this experience.*

- This step helps the writers reflect on their lives and decide what's been difficult, past or present (today, last week, last year, many years ago). It also helps in organizing their thoughts, specifying emotions, and knowing where to begin the next step (#3).

Step 3: Imagine. *Choose one challenging experience in your life (it can be one that you wrote about in Step 2). Tell the story of that experience by beginning each sentence in your story with the word Imagine. Start with your first memory—what do your heart and mind think of first, when you consider that experience? Continue writing until you are done telling the story. You may find a natural shift, moving into the positive side of the story; if not, you can write this in step 4. This is free writing so don't worry about spelling, grammar, punctuation, or sentence structure for now.*

- This "free writing" instruction applies to the first draft, to encourage kids to simply get their thoughts and feelings on paper. Editing for grammar, punctuation, and sentence structure can happen later.
- Writing an *Imagine* story can be difficult for some writers. They may feel vulnerable, and most children don't like to feel exposed, weak, or awkward. Vulnerability, however, is key to processing difficult life circumstances and moving

forward (Brown, 2013). It helps to remind writers that it's perfectly normal and okay for them to feel vulnerable, which you might describe for them as feeling silly, shy, embarrassed, unsure, as well as exposed, weak, or awkward. Remind them not to worry about spelling and grammar, or making it perfect.

- While they write, playing soft music at low volume may help them feel emotionally calm and safe. Go to www.theimagineproject.org to download the Lesson Plans for age-appropriate suggestions about music.

- Reassure them that no one else has to read it if they don't want them to. It is important to honor this—if you tell them you won't read it—don't read it. They may let you read it in time, but they will write more if they can trust that no one else will see it. If they don't ever let you read it, that's okay too, and an important part of their process.

- Some kids won't know where to start. To give them an encouraging nudge, I always say, "Begin where your heart wants to speak." I often give examples from my own life or read *Imagine* stories from the book.

- Encourage younger or less experienced writers to write with detail and break up one Imagine sentence into many. Some kids may focus only on the events that happened, so remind them to also write down how they felt and to describe what each moment was like for them. For example, a 2nd grade girl wrote, "*Imagine... falling off a ride at Elitches (an amusement park) and breaking your arm." I encouraged her to write *Imagine* statements that also described the park, the ride, how she fell off, what it felt like after the fall, and going to the doctor, to make it more complete and create a deeper meaning for her. You may have to give some examples of how to break down each part of the story, use creative words, and add emotional content to make the story more clear, full, and interesting.

- Some writers will find a natural shift from the negative to the positive as they write, while others will need encouragement to move to the positive, which is step 4.
- Have them continue to write as long as they are willing (some need 10 minutes, some need 30 or more).

Step 4: Possibilities. *Now it's time to imagine new possibilities in your life. What is the ending you would like to have to your Imagine story? Dream big—imagine what you want to do in your life!*

- This is a critical step in helping the writers determine what they want instead of their old story. This is the most powerful part of the process, as imagining what is possible gives them hope, drives them forward, and empowers them!
- As humans, we have a hard time knowing what we want—many just say, "I want to be happy," unless they are asked to define what will make them happy. This step pushes writers to think

about what they really want in life; who they are, what they can do, be, and find purpose in.

- Give them a wide variety of age-appropriate examples. Kids from different cultures and socioeconomic backgrounds may have very different dreams.

- Many kids have dreams that may not be realistic (such as playing a professional sport), but that's okay! Let them dream whatever they want. The sky is the limit! It's fun and still useful for them to Imagine any new possibilities in their lives. Besides, if they commit themselves to it, anything is possible—but they have to define it first!

Step 5: I am, I can, I will. *Own your dreams by transforming your* Imagine *dreams into "I" statements, such as, I am..., I can..., I will....* On the bottom of the page, write the emotions you will feel when you accomplish these dreams.

- This step is important because it grounds their new *Imagines* into action plans, and turns them into concrete visions for themselves. This also helps them own their dreams and believe they can make their dreams happen. In the classroom, I often encourage kids stand and say these statements out loud with power behind them. You can have your children/students write their "I" statements on balloons and watch them expand as they blow them up bigger and bigger. It's a fun activity and adds playfulness into the mix.

Step 6: Do. *Name three things you need to do to make your dreams happen.*

- Kids often wish and even believe that life will just show up on their doorstep without any work or effort. This step shows the writers that it requires work to make their Imagine dreams come true!
- Encourage the kids to be realistic such as studying more, getting better grades, getting enough sleep, hanging out with the right people, or showing up to class!

Step 7: The 30-Day Imagine, Gratitude, and Kindness Challenge. *Every day for 30 days, write three things you want to Imagine in your life, three things you are grateful for, and do one act of kindness every day.*

- Doing anything for at least 21 days creates a new habit. Helping kids create the habit of *Imagining* their futures, finding gratitude in each day, and being kind will help them in so many ways. Research shows that goal-setting is key to being successful in making your dreams happen. Gratitude has been studied extensively and keeping daily gratitude changes the brain in ways that improve well-being. Teaching kindness is essential to creating a softer, more compassionate home, classroom, community, and world.
- As a parent or teacher, you can try incentives to help kids stay consistent for 30 days, and even do it with them and compare. It's fun to *Imagine* what it will be like when you achieve the goals you want, or to imagine where you'll be in 5 or 10 or 20

years. It's also a good game to play when you have some free time with your children or students.

How Many Stories Should They Write?

My dream/goal for *My Imagine Journal* is that it be a tool everyone can use as often as needed. Encouraging kids to do this kind of writing daily, or whenever they are faced with emotional challenges, can continue to benefit their physical and emotional health. In fact, children have multiple stories to tell, and sometimes they have to tell a few softer stories before they feel safe telling the ones that go deep, though sometimes the bigger stories come out immediately. Experiment and see what works best.

How Do I Write and Share an *Imagine* Story?

You too can write a story and share it with your children/students—doing so can be a profound experience for all of you. If you share your story, be sure to choose a topic that is age-appropriate. *Be mindful about sharing the details of your experience, as sharing a trauma will put your children / students at risk for secondary trauma.* Patty, whose story is in the back of this book, wrote a story about her own teenage son who was struggling with drugs and getting into trouble. When her son read the story, he was profoundly shifted because he realized what kind of impact his behavior was having on his mom. Teachers who share stories tell me that students love hearing more about teacher's lives; it also strengthens teacher-student relationships by creating more trust and compassion. The goal is to show kids that they are not alone in facing challenges, and they too can prevail and become successful grown-ups like you have done. Do this wisely and gently, and kids will LOVE hearing stories from your own childhood!

What to Write About

- Daily stressors or significant stress in the past or present
- Loss, illness, death, grief
- The hardest thing you've been through
- Something that happened at school or work that bothers you
- An assignment or specific class you disliked
- A teacher/boss who was challenging you
- Challenges with friends or social media
- Something that frequently worries you
- How you dealt with a difficult relationship
- Family challenges, such as parents arguing, siblings struggling, financial woes, moving, illness, or divorce.

Reading the Stories Aloud

As a parent, encourage your child to read their story out loud to you. It will be powerful for both of you! In the classroom, I always ask kids and teens if anyone wants to read their story aloud. There is power in reading your story to others; it's about owning who you are, your story, and your resilience. Many kids don't want to read them out loud, but many do. Again, the most important thing is that they feel safe as they read them—having a close relationship with someone in the room can feel supportive to the reader. As a parent, teacher, or counselor, it's imperative to acknowledge their stories without judgment and with compassion. Giving them a hug (if appropriate), looking in their eyes and saying, "Wow, that must have been hard," and in a classroom, showing respect by having the other kids applaud at the end. You might be concerned about having some stories read in front of other kids, and fear bullying or teasing. Honestly, in my experience, these stories have brought out the opposite reaction. Kids are so compassionate; they feel sorry for each other and take strength in each other's stories at the same time. In fact, it's a good time for a lesson in empathy—to show kids what to do to help a vulnerable child who might need extra positive attention later. The kids always pull through with compassion, and it's beautiful to witness. *The Imagine Project* fosters the understanding that everyone has a story. It inspires kids to believe that if someone else survived such hardship, they can do it too. Camaraderie develops and new friendships grow between children and teens who have similar stories.

For the Listener. It's important to be a kind and nonjudgmental listener. Sometimes you might grapple with your own emotions. It can be hard to listen to difficult stories, particularly if it's your own child's story, and/or if there are a lot of them in a classroom or group setting. To resist taking on the stories yourself, remember, it's not your job to fix them; it's your job to listen and let them process, let it go, and become more resilient in the process. I often have to remind myself it's my job to see each child without his/her story. It's my job to see them as the resilient, amazing people they are between the lines they write. It's my job to honor the value of each journey, rather than second-guessing it and the lessons it holds. These are your jobs too.

When the Stories are Emotional. When we are writing about difficult times in our lives, it's easy to become emotional. This is common with expressive writing and it might last for a few minutes, a few hours, or until we get a good night's sleep. This is normal and an important part of the process of releasing emotions that are tied up with the story. It's difficult to see kids cry; we want to fix their problems and dry their tears. Instead, let them cry—it's okay. Some sort of genuine reassurance may help (hug, look in their eyes with compassion, touching their shoulder), but truly, listening with compassion is a soothing balm. If you feel the need to do more, here's a trick that will help both you and the children/students to calm down. Do this with the kids:

- Have them put their hands on their legs, right hand on their right leg, left hand on their left leg.
- Have them tap their legs with their fingers, back and forth, alternating legs; tap on the right leg with the right hand and then on the left leg with their left hand, in a rhythm back and forth.
- They can also cross their arms and tap under their arms, back and forth, or they can cross their arms over their heart and tap back and forth on their shoulders; whatever they are comfortable with.
- Keep tapping as long as they need to calm down— 5 to 7 minutes should do.

Tapping will help the listeners too. You can even do this while they listen to the stories being read. Tapping balances the brain, reducing the level of stress hormones in the body and producing a neutral emotional state—a great trick to keep in your back pocket! (Read chapter 11 for more information about tapping.)

Family Imagines

Imagine your child writing about thoughts he or she hasn't been able to share with you. Imagine knowing what is really going through their minds. Imagine them reading your story and understanding you more than they ever did before. Imagine this happening as a family—how close it can bring all of you.

Try writing *Imagine* stories as a family, particularly when you are dealing with some underlying obvious or mysterious challenges. Your child may not be able to say what they feel, but they may be able to write it down. They might not be able to share it right away, but at some point, when they feel safe, they may share it. Don't pressure them to share, but show them an *Imagine* story of yours that is appropriate for a young audience. (See "How Do I Write and Share an Imagine Story?" earlier in this chapter.) Sharing some of yours will bring them closer to you and may make them feel safer sharing their stories when they are ready.

Michelle Parker, a teacher to 5th grade students, says, "After doing *The Imagine Project*, I hear my students saying to someone who is having a bad day, or is sad or mad about something, 'Imagine it getting better!' I think they are learning to grasp that they may go through tough times, but they can influence what happens next. They are also more compassionate, aren't as quick to judge, and they are comfortable and confident sharing their written stories with each other now. The best part—because of *The Imagine Project* they LOVE TO WRITE—EVERYTHING!"

Tips for Teachers

The Imagine Project supports social and emotional health in the classroom as well as other environments, such as the school bus, hallways, cafeteria, and playgrounds. When kids are given the opportunity to speak about something that is bothering them and/or causing them emotional distress, they begin to understand their own emotions better and they become more resilient, confident, content, focused, patient, less judgmental, and kinder to others. Hearing other student's stories helps kids realize they are not alone, that there are others around them who have been through similar circumstances and survived, so they can too. Students learn to have compassion for strangers and understand that everyone has a story.

In a room of about 50 7th graders, one student read a story about himself and his mom having Type I Diabetes; he wrote about how hard it was for both of them. As the class bully listened to this story he was overheard saying, "Wow, I will never tease him about that again, I didn't know it was so hard!" Hearing the story gave him a new perspective of empathy, kindness, and understanding.

By using *My Imagine Journal* and its seven-step process, students have the opportunity to use creative writing skills and imagination to enhance their social emotional growth by:

- developing a healthy awareness of their own emotional needs
- understanding resilience
- improving citizenship by considering the perspective of others
- developing interpersonal relationship skills and awareness
- improving academic performance
- preventing maladaptive behaviors

Teachers can incorporate *The Imagine Project* into their literacy curriculums and certain national, state, and district standards can be met. Those standards include, but aren't limited to:

- reading, writing, and speaking skills
- providing social and emotional support
- supporting affective learning
- offering decision-making opportunities
- encouraging higher-level thinking
- supporting interpersonal skills
- taking action to achieve goals

The Imagine Project has no-cost journals for teachers to use (see www.theimagineproject.org). There are three journals, designed to be developmentally appropriate for different age groups. Each journal guides students through the seven steps, which are best completed over a series of days or even weeks. The *Kindergarten through 2nd Grade* journal follows the children's book, *Byron the Caterpillar Who Loved to Imagine* (Yampa Valley Publishing, 2017). It's not until about 2nd grade that most children understand the concept of beginning a sentence with the word *Imagine*. Instead, reading about *Byron* teaches messages about listening to your heart, believing in yourself, and kindness to others. The journal then asks them follow-up questions, helping younger students think about life more deeply, similar to the journals for the older students, but without the Imagine stories. The *Grades 3 to 5* journal can be used as young as you feel confident using it. The younger students who are just learning how to write sentences will need more one-on-one support; the journaling can also be done orally or by drawing.

Here are some more tips specific to using *My Imagine Journal* in the classroom:

- There are Lesson Plans at www.theimagineproject. org/journals to follow, if needed.
- Spread kids out in the classroom, for example, letting them sit on the floor or someplace away from their friends so they aren't easily distracted.
- Use your professional judgment to scaffold the writing as necessary, allowing students to write in their primary language or use drawings to

accomplish the task. Drawing prior to writing may be important for some students to help them keep their information constant in time and space; they can refer back to the drawing to organize their thinking and writing.

- A simple graphic organizer can help students get their ideas down on paper. You can have a word list and or pictures to help students with limited vocabulary.

- Focus primarily on content and the meaning students are communicating first, not on the surface features or grammar, spelling, or punctuation. Editing can be done later in the process if it's necessary for a bigger project such as an autobiography.

- For kids who resist or can't write, consider using technology such as voice to text, video apps, adult dictation, or telling their *Imagines* to someone they trust.

- Students in 4th and 5th grades seem to especially enjoy writing and reading their *Imagine* stories. Middle-schoolers can be resistant but once they hear others' stories (from their classroom or in the books), they typically soften and may even love writing. Ninth grade is also a very good year to use the project as these students are transitioning to high school and may have many challenges. But really, it can be valuable in any grade, as most middle school and high school kids love to talk about themselves, which makes them receptive to doing the project.

- Imagine groups/clubs can be created in schools, led by a teacher or student.
- If you are concerned about a student's story, have the student see the school counselor or psychologist. Follow school and district policies when utilizing such resources.
- Using *The Imagine Project* in the classroom often brings kids closer together. Sharing as a whole group is powerful but also can be effective in pairs or small groups.
- Writing and sharing an *Imagine* story of your own may also boost classroom camaraderie. If you are comfortable with doing this, the kids will love hearing it!
- There are videos on www.theimagineproject.org to inspire kids to write their *Imagine* stories.
- Knowing your student's stories will help you be aware of the underlying issues students are dealing with so you can better support them in learning.
- *The Imagine Project* helps build relationships between the teachers and students because it promotes greater understanding of the students' lives outside the classroom. It can be used with other programs that support social-emotional learning, such as conflict resolution, restorative justice, and No-Nonsense Nurturing.
- Be patient with students who don't want to write their stories. Some just can't find the words. Others aren't ready to divulge information about themselves. If they adamantly refuse, you

can have them write an *Imagine* story about a historical figure, their favorite character in a book, or anyone they admire, such as a celebrity in music, acting, or sports. Or they can do other homework. After they hear other kids' stories, they may feel inspired or motivated to write their own. Accept each child's pace and timetable for writing their *Imagine* story.

- Even after you have done *The Imagine Project* in your classroom, whenever a student is struggling at home, socially, or even academically, you can continue to use *The Imagine Project* process to help them express their emotions or frustrations, and set intentions for behavior. Keep a few printed journals on hand, perhaps in "the calming corner," as an option for students.

At first glance, teachers and administrators often worry that doing the journaling process will be heavy and hard for students (and teachers), but in most cases, it's not as difficult as you might think. Instead, it's profound and inspiring. Will there be tears? Probably, and that's okay—what a wonderful way to show kids that expressing emotion is permitted and appropriate. What most kids need during this process is a compassionate adult who sees them with a caring heart, hugs them if it's appropriate, and gives reassurance that they will be okay. With that said, some students may need extra support from a trained specialist, for example, a school counselor, psychologist, or social worker. Teachers can benefit from training on how to support students who are feeling big or complicated emotions.

Even for kids who don't like to write, many love using *My Imagine Journal*. They have so much to say and so few avenues to speak what's in their hearts. Creating a habit of journaling to *Imagine* their futures can be critical to their social, emotional, and academic success in life.

Ultimately, *The Imagine Project* is about teaching students they don't have to be held back by the negative stories in their lives. Instead they can *Imagine* and pursue whatever they want, always working to move forward and not letting the bumps in the road of life get in the way.

PART THREE

Sustaining Emotional Wellness by Nurturing the Mind, Body, and Spirit

WRITING WITH *MY IMAGINE JOURNAL*™ IS A powerful process. It can bring major shifts in perspectives on life, as well as profound emotional growth. It's important, however, to continually nurture the body, mind, and spirit in order to maintain emotional wellness. This section gives you more tools to help your children or students—and you—seek contentment and maintain a joyful life that keeps moving forward.

These additional tools are wide-ranging and go beyond Western medicine, which has its limits. I learned very quickly as a nurse and as mother to Mackenzie, who was chronically sick for years after her premature birth, that complete healing doesn't happen by treating issues only by Western medical labels and addressing only the symptoms. Western medicine is helpful and sometimes critical to use, but often incomplete. Caring for Mackenzie who was on oxygen for three and a half years, tube fed for four years, needed occupational, physical, and speech therapy weekly, as well as IV infusions monthly for four years, taught me to look beyond what Western medical doctors might recommend and find other ways to help her and myself. Along the way, I became an expert in what's available in both Western *and* alternative or "complementary," medical therapies. I believe it was the combination of both Western and complementary therapies that brought Mackenzie to be the healthy and successful person she is today. Can you tell I'm a proud momma?!

The following chapters offer many options for holistically boosting emotional wellness, which fosters your child's ability to manage drama, trauma, and stress.

Some options will resonate with you, and some may not. Something may work for one child but not for another. Try what makes sense and feels comfortable; maybe try something that is new to you. Educate yourself, experiment, and determine the best avenues for helping each child—and yourself—overcome obstacles and succeed in life.

6

NURTURING THE MIND

IMAGINE
STORY
by Dylan,
12ᵗʰ grade
Alternative School
Program

Imagine...being 15 years old and being the worst kid ever.

Imagine...tearing down a relationship with your family and loved ones because of your old man's abusive characteristics.

Imagine...always getting into trouble, ditching days and weeks of school, not caring about anything or anyone.

Imagine...always thinking about how poorly your father treated you as a kid.

Imagine...being afraid to tell anyone ever about a mental condition you were born with.

Imagine...using chemicals and self-hatred to try and wash your pain away.

Imagine...not telling anyone about yourself because they will judge your past and not see your happy polite self.

Imagine...wanting to dig yourself out of your depression, risking your life for it.

Imagine...meeting new friends for the first time.

Imagine...meeting the love of your life.

Imagine...finally making amends with your dad and watching him improve as a person.

Imagine...being 20 ½ years old, doing your best to finally finish high school and get out of the house again.

WHEN WE THINK ABOUT HEALING, MANY OF US focus only on our physical bodies. In reality, there is a great deal of research showing our minds lead the way for our bodies. What we think drives what we do, how we behave, and how we interact. Our thoughts even affect our cellular structure. Scientists used to believe that the body was made up of only physical matter; it functioned in specific ways and was only affected by other matter such as chemical responses (medications), surgery, and other physical modalities. Now we know the body is more than matter—it's energy, and can be affected by many things, particularly the mind.

In his book, *The Biology of Belief*, Bruce Lipton writes, "Thoughts, the mind's energy, directly influence how the physical brain controls the body's physiology. Thought 'energy' can activate or inhibit the cell's function..." In other words, thoughts can control the health of both the mind and the body. Using the mind to help handle drama, trauma, and stress is the key to emotional wellness. Here are some useful tools to help your children's/students' minds cope with life.

Mindfulness

Mindfulness is about being fully aware of what is happening in the present moment, both internally and externally. It's a conscious decision to pay attention to your body, mind, emotions, and external circumstances, and to do so from a nonjudgmental place—a place of noticing and letting go of anything that doesn't serve you. This may sound challenging, and it can be at times, but the more you practice the easier it gets. For kids, the earlier they learn these habits, the greater the impact.

According to research on mindfulness with adults and with children, mindfulness improves immune function (fewer illnesses), increases concentration, and decreases stress. There is a long list of positive effects on children who practice mindfulness.

THE BENEFITS OF PRACTICING
MINDFULNESS FOR KIDS

- Self-acceptance
- Compassion for themselves and others
- Strengthened resilience
- Better focus and concentration at school and at home
- Increased happiness/joy
- Increased self-esteem
- Improved social skills
- Decreased anxiety, depression, and other painful emotions
- Better control of anger and hyperactivity
- Improved sleep

Many who teach mindfulness advocate that it begins with paying attention to your breath. In calm moments, or in times of distress, bring your attention back to your breath, and practice long, slow, mindful breathing. This is key to embracing the moment and restoring or strengthening calm in your brain and body. In her book, *Rising Strong*, Brené Brown writes about her "calm practice" in which "breathing is central to practicing mindfulness." You can try it by sitting quietly and gently paying attention to your breath, counting slowly as you breathe in and out. The goal is breathing in to a count of about 6 or 7, and the same breathing out. You may have to work at going this slow, but just try it at your own pace and work at moving to a slower, deeper breath. Then practice at other times too, in your car, waiting in a doctor's office, or watching TV. The more you experiment and work at it, the more prepared you'll be when you really need it to calm yourself in stressful situations!

Practicing Mindfulness with Kids and Teens

Practicing mindfulness with kids can begin during the early weeks of a pregnancy, which is an important time of brain growth. Sitting quietly for a time each day, perhaps reading or listening to music, can program your unborn baby's biology, and reduce susceptibility to emotional problems early in life. With newborns, take time to just sit and rock, sing, read, and enjoy your baby. Be very present and not distracted by other things around you. As your babies grow into children, continue with quiet times—no phone, no TV, no distractions, just you and your children experiencing and talking about life.

You may need to be creative to help your growing child with mindfulness. Here are some ideas:

- Sit together and have a snack. Talk about the snack and its characteristics; your favorite flavor, its texture, its temperature. Really noticing what you're eating helps you be in the moment instead of worrying about anything else. To be playful, make funny faces to show your opinion of a food, or come up with creative ideas for weird meals.
- Do a puzzle together.
- Go for a walk and talk about the trees, birds, bugs, or grass.

- Read a book together. Talk about the book and what you both thought about the story and characters.
- Ask your child about the weather inside their hearts—sunny, cloudy, bright, rainy, or stormy. Be curious about their day and its highs and lows.
- Write your *Imagine* stories together.
- Play a game, anything from peek-a-boo and hide-and-go-seek to card games or board games.
- Cook together.
- Chase bubbles.
- Look at the clouds and find formations in them.
- Pick a country on the world map and research it.
- Draw, color, create together.
- Tell a story at bedtime, real or fictional.

Any one of these activities needs to be your full focus for at least 15 minutes, even longer can be better; no distractions, just one-on-one attention while you are being mindful of the present moment. The above suggestions are forms of mindfulness you can do together. If your kids are up for it, you can sit quietly and listen to a meditation together, maybe someday they will do it on their own! What a great way to do something together that is peaceful and helpful.

I met a wonderful woman recently. Roni Wing Lambrecht is the author of Parenting at your Best: Powerful Reflections and Straightforward Tips for Becoming a Mindful Parent. *Roni lost her only child, Dalton, in a tragic accident when he was 15 years old. She has incredible strength and has used her tragic loss to help others.*

Roni told me a story about a recent trip to one of her husband's favorite restaurants to pick up take-out. As she stood in an unusually long line and waited to pick up her order, she looked around the restaurant and noticed a family of four eat in silence as they engaged with their phones. Roni watched them for over 20 minutes—they never spoke to one another. By the time she picked up her food and reached the counter to pay, she was in tears and could barely speak. All she could think about was how she would give anything to have one last meal with her son, while those parents were throwing away their time with their family, teaching their kids that it was okay to do so. Roni decided to purchase a dessert for them to share, with a note, explaining how she had lost her son and would give anything to have this dessert to share with him. In the note, she asked them to remember that every moment is precious, and to please spend it communicating with each other, rather than wasting a single moment. Lastly, she asked them to Pay It Forward in her son's memory.

Wow! Imagine the wake-up call the family at the restaurant had! Roni's book has brilliant advice on being a mindful parent and how to value the time that is a gift for you, and a gift for your children. Please make use of every moment you have with your loved ones. There are a few great books written for parents to help their children with mindfulness practices. See "References and Resources" at the back of this book for more recommendations.

Gratitude

Gratitude is so simple, yet most people overlook it's amazing benefits. Dr. David Hamilton, author of *Why Kindness is Good for You*, writes, "Gratitude is a mark of being kind to life by being aware of all that is around us, and when we are grateful, we acknowledge the people and situations in our life and express thanks for them." We teach our children to say "thank you," but it's also important to model and teach them to see gratitude as a key philosophy of life. Seeing and feeling gratitude every day is one key to being resilient and successful.

There is quite a bit of research on gratitude and the positive effects. These positive effects make sense, because when you think about what you feel grateful for, you can't help but feel relaxed, fulfilled, and blessed.

THE BENEFITS OF GRATITUDE

- Greater sense of well-being
- Improved physical health
- Improved self-esteem, resilience, and empathy
- Decreased aggression
- Increased optimism
- Improved sleep

Gratitude even improves relationships. Research shows that saying thank you to someone helps to create a more positive relationship. When a child feels gratitude from his or her parents for being helpful or for just being a good kid, the child feels safer and more empowered to say something when they are upset and need to talk.

It is fairly easy to teach kids to practice a life philosophy of gratitude. Using the *30-day Imagine, Gratitude, and Kindness Challenge* (Step 7 in *My Imagine Journal*) is a good place to start. Kids can have fun creating a family gratitude board or a gratitude box where everyone can write, keep, and even share what they feel grateful for.

We play *The Gratitude Game* in the car or at mealtime. Particularly if someone has had a bad day, this can help them put it in perspective and feel better.

THE GRATITUDE GAME

Each person takes a turn saying what they are grateful for, beginning with, "I am grateful for...". You can also use, "I love..." saying what you love about each person or life in general!

Everyone takes at least three turns. If someone is unhappy about something, it may help to first clear the air by letting them talk about what's upsetting them, while others listen with compassion. After they've had their say, feel more relaxed, and are ready to change perspective, switch it to gratitude, and watch moods brighten.

If someone wants to remain cranky, it might feel like pulling teeth to get them to join the game, but be patient and gently invite them to join when they feel ready. They may be content to listen—and benefit from it—especially if they know it's not being done to manipulate their mood. Even if they continue to resist, simply let them be, and honor their desire to come around in their own time, on their own terms.

Kindness

It feels good to be kind. It's in our nature to be kind, but we have to teach and cultivate it in ourselves and our children. Kindness not only benefits others, it has positive effects on our bodies and our minds.

Research has shown that doing acts of kindness

- makes us happier,
- improves immune function,
- changes chemical balance in the brain to reduce depression,
- releases oxytocin (a happy hormone!),
- decreases inflammation in the body, improving our health,
- helps us feel better about ourselves,
- Decreases bullying,
- increases peer acceptance, and
- is contagious.

Talking to your children about being kind is important, but kids learn what they see, so the more they witness and experience kindness, the more they will practice it themselves. Step 7 in *My Imagine Journal* encourages one random act of kindness every day for 30 days—a great way to ingrain a kindness philosophy into a child's life. There are hundreds of simple acts of kindness to show and teach kids, www.kindness.org has great ideas. Here are some to begin with:

- Write a thank you card.
- Let someone go ahead of you in line.
- Carry something for someone who needs help.
- Tell someone why they are special to you.

- Talk to someone new at school.
- Donate food or clothing.
- At a restaurant or store, tell an employee what a good job they did for you.
- Pick up litter.
- Help make dinner.
- Write a poem for a friend.
- Talk to a lonely neighbor.
- Play with a pet (you might even go to an animal shelter and play with the animals there).
- Give your mom a neck or shoulder massage. ☺

Intention

An intention is the starting point of every new possibility in life. We often imagine and dream of different or better things for ourselves, but when asked, many kids (and adults) aren't really sure what they want to have, be, or do. "I want to be happy!" is a common answer, but it's not a clear goal. In order to create more, different, or better in life, it's important to think about specifics. This is a life skill we can teach our children; it will benefit them now and in the future.

An intention is a clear and positive goal regarding what you want to have and experience in life. If you have a distinct end in mind, your thoughts, actions, attitude, and choices will move in that direction. If you don't have a distinct end in mind, you will stumble and wander without direction. Research has proven that defined intentions and goals reap greater success in many areas of life, including education. The trick is understanding what you want.

Imagining new possibilities in life is a great conversation starter with kids. It can be fun, interesting, and exciting. You can use the word *Imagine* if you'd like.

Imagine...traveling the world.
Imagine...swimming with dolphins.
Imagine...going to college.

Ideas can be endless, but intention is necessary to make them real. When an idea comes to your child's mind (or yours), help them move forward and set some intentions as to when and how they will realize them. Ask what it will look, feel, smell, even taste like if that fits. Embellishing an idea makes it even more real and they will work harder to achieve it.

Encourage your kids to write down or draw their *Imagines* on a piece of paper and put it somewhere they can see it. Visibility will spur them to think about it often, envision it, and feel good about the new possibility. Even scenarios that seem impossible can be helpful, as feeling hopeful can give them energy to muscle through difficult times.

Intuition

Intuition is not talked about often, but we all have it and we all feel it from time to time. I believe I've dodged a few potentially dangerous situations because I listened to my gut. I made it a point to teach my kids to listen to their intuition, particularly if they are in situations where they aren't sure what to do. My middle son loves extreme sports. When he's headed up to the top of a mountain to ski terrain most skiers won't even consider, he always reassures me that he'll follow his gut feeling on where and how to ski down. He's intelligent and knowledgeable about back country skiing, but he also depends on his intuition. My daughter recently told me that at a gas station, she saw a man who didn't seem right. Her gut told her to stay in the car; she did and left. Intuition is a key component of life and trusting it is a must to teach your children.

What is intuition? There is a part of us that just knows more than what our conscious minds can evaluate. Some call it our higher self, some might say it's God showing us the way, some believe it's angels or the soul talking. But recent brain research reveals that intuition can be the result of specific brain activity. Outside of your conscious awareness, your brain constantly takes in vast amounts of information as it scans the environment or a situation. And as explained in chapter 2, it continually responds by releasing hormones that either maintain your calm or launch you into a stress reaction. Whatever you think intuition is, you'd be wise to listen to it—and teach your kids to listen to it—as it's typically right on the mark!

How can you use intuition? Listening to your intuition means paying attention not only to what your head thinks, but what your body feels. When you think about doing something and your body (mainly your chest and stomach) feels soft, light, comfortable, or easy, then it's the right thing to do. In contrast, when thinking about it makes you feel tense, tight, uncomfortable, and unsure, then don't do it. Why? Because the tension in your body is triggered by your limbic system, which is pumping stress hormones into your blood stream at the prospect of making the wrong move. Your thinking brain or conscious mind may be unaware of the potential, but your body can feel the effects of your brain's assessment. So tune into how your body feels. Another way of saying this is "listen to your gut," which is considered to be our "second mind."

So if you're detecting a tense reaction in your body when doing something or making a decision, either go the other way or delay the decision until you can think through what you need or want to do. If what you are facing is stressful, really listen to your gut and ask yourself what the next step might be, and if you should keep going with what you are doing. Keep listening and you will figure it out. If at any time you feel clearly uncertain and uncomfortable with a situation, consider moving in the other direction.

What can you teach children about intuition? The first step is to teach children how to tune into their bodily sensations. (*See below for an important cautionary note.*) Ask them to imagine something happy and talk about how that feels in the body. Then move to other emotions like excitement, sadness, fear, worry, shame, and anger. Not only does this teach emotional self-awareness, but also gets them in touch with what their gut is telling them about a particular decision, person, or situation. Talk to them about making decisions not only with their minds, but with their gut feelings too. Teach them that when they feel easy and comfortable with a decision to follow it, and when they feel tense and unsure to wait or do something different.

Of course, sometimes we are fooled, such as when we make fearful assumptions about unfamiliar situations or people who look different from us. But it can pay to listen to your intuition, especially when you have persistent or mysterious physical symptoms, or there is a gnawing sense in your gut that "something isn't right." In contrast, when you're feeling effortlessly calm, excited, or happy, you can bet that this sense of ease indicates that you're on a good path or perhaps in the right place, at the right time, or with the right people.

Please note that it is inadvisable to do body-awareness exercises with children who are suffering from untreated, moderate to severe trauma, as tuning into their hypervigilant, stressed-to-the-max bodies can create an acute crisis. These children first require professional, brain-based treatment for their trauma. However, for only mildly- to moderately-stressed children, guided body awareness can be safe. Do stay attuned to each child and back off or provide another activity whenever a child doesn't want to explore or play along with body-awareness exercises.

Laughter

Our world is too serious, too often. We may be so overwhelmed with life that we don't take enough time to laugh. Yet, there is scientific evidence that laughter positively affects our bodies and brains. Laughter relaxes muscles, improves breathing, and raises pain thresholds. It releases dopamine and other hormones that make us feel happy, and decreases stress, anxiety, depression, and gives us an overall feeling of wellness. There is nothing better than a good belly laugh!

Finding laughter throughout the day will help anyone at any age. Kids often laugh much easier than adults. Try to make laughter part of your family's life as often as possible. Tell jokes, be silly, dance around the room, make faces, tickle, watch funny videos, shows, or movies. Everyone laughs about different things; find what works for you and your kids.

Optimism

Optimism is a mindset. Optimistic people see the positive side of things. Some people are naturally optimistic—they are just born that way—but it's also something kids learn through experiences and watching those around them. Regardless of how negative someone is, they can learn to be more optimistic.

Optimistic people are more successful, resilient, less stressed, and actually live longer. Here are a few tips to help kids be more optimistic:

- Recognize when they are successful and remark about it; refrain from negative remarks about times when they are not successful.
- Help them be successful by having them do things you know they will succeed in. Set them up for success by giving them the tools and teaching them the skills they need.
- When things go wrong, acknowledge their feelings; once they've moved through the disappointment, talk about the good that might have come out of the situation.
- Help them reframe failure as an opportunity to learn and grow.

- Ward off pessimistic thinking habits by encouraging positive thinking habits. For example, instead of "Something is wrong with me," say, "That was a difficult task. I need more help/a new set of skills/better tools." Instead of, "I'll never succeed," say, "I will be better prepared and try harder next time." Instead of, "All tests are hard," say, "That test was hard." Instead of, "I never pass tests," say, "I didn't pass the test yesterday."
- Don't label kids negatively—give them positive labels. For example, say, "energetic" not "hyperactive;" "sensitive" not "moody;" or "bright, inquisitive, and enthusiastic" not "troublemaker."
- Watch your own words—keep them as positive as possible.
- Be optimistic yourself—you know the old saying "Fake it until you make it." Do your best to be realistically positive.

My son, Frank, has a silly game he uses to stay positive called, "The Opposite of That". When he has a sore throat he will call me and say, "Mom, my throat feels awesome, but the opposite of that!" or when he's running out of money he will say, "I have so much money in my account, but the opposite of that!" Try it sometime, it's kind of fun, especially with kids, and it feels much better than just stating the negative truth.

Tips for Teachers

As teachers, you know there is so much more to a quality education than reading, writing, and arithmetic. Although you are often bound by testing and reaching required district standards, you also want to inspire and teach students how to survive, thrive, and make a difference in the world. Helping their minds relax, enjoy, embrace others, and appreciate are all important in teaching a developing mind. Here are some classrooms tips to help you help your students expand their perceptions of life.

- Start with your own mindfulness practice, as this gives you ownership and comfort implementing mindfulness with your students.
- Establish daily mindfulness routines for students to become familiar with. You'll start to see them use these on their own.
- See www.mindfulschools.org for great audio and visual aids. Also go to www.mindfulteachers.org for practical tips and tricks to implement in the classroom.
- Keep a daily or weekly gratitude journal with your students. Using *My Imagine Journal* is a great place to start.
- Create a class tree or mural of some kind, to which students can add daily or weekly gratitudes.
- Have students write (and/or say) their intentions for the day, week, or even school year.
- Encourage kindness by exuding kindness. Also acknowledge students when they have been kind and encourage students to speak up when they witness a kind act toward themselves or someone else.

- Set aside time to have a good laugh. Just laugh—this is a good trick to release emotions. Tell jokes, watch a funny video, or even do laughter yoga. (I've never tried it, but it sounds fun!) Laughter is good medicine!

7

NURTURING THE BODY

IMAGINE
STORY
by Julen,
age 17
(written with his
mom, Michelle)

*Imagine…*hitting every pediatric milestone just like you're supposed to.

*Imagine…*being labeled with severe learning disabilities at age 3.

*Imagine…*your parents feeling guilty for speaking to you in two languages, thinking that was why you were not talking.

Imagine… spending hours in therapy, changing your diet, taking 75 compounded vitamins daily… trying to make a difference.

*Imagine…*facing new social and academic challenges with each phase of development.

Imagine...having your teacher tell your parents that you will not be able to get a job or live independently.

Imagine...your parents making the decision to focus on what you can do, rather than on what you cannot do.

Imagine...NOT LETTING LABELS AND LIMITATIONS DEFINE WHO YOU ARE.

Imagine...the power of making choices based on THAT core belief.

Imagine...the sense of accomplishment once you are able to speak to both sets of grandparents: one in English and one in Spanish.

Imagine...realizing you have a true passion for cooking and turning that passion into productivity.

Imagine...developing and starting your own sauce business at age 16.

Imagine...Batching, bottling, labeling, packaging and selling these sauces in grocery stores and online.

Imagine...working in a restaurant preparing the sauce you created, and having that sauce featured on the menu.

Imagine...your dream is to grow your business so that you can employ other people with special needs.

Imagine...not for one minute thinking you are any different than anyone else.

Imagine...Starting each day believing that it will be the best day ever.

(Julen Ucar is the creator of *Julen's Ausome Sauce*)

PHYSICAL HEALTH AND EMOTIONAL HEALTH are more interrelated than many people realize. Just as emotional wellness promotes good physical health, keeping our bodies (and brains!) healthy can help prevent, even heal, emotional issues. Here are some ideas to help you and your child stay physically *and* emotionally healthy using the basics such as exercise, nutrition, sleep, but also adding some ideas to make life interesting and fun!

Exercise

Today's kids just don't move enough—they spend way more time in front of a screen than previous generations did. So helping your child learn to weave daily exercise into a healthy lifestyle is an important part of a parent's job. Children typically follow the example of their parents, extended family, or friends. So modeling this habit yourself can make a big impression!

Exercise is important because it helps improve mood, self-esteem, self-image, quality of sleep, attention, academic performance, interpersonal skills, and coordination, while creating a strong healthy body. All of these are important when coping with stress and trauma.

Some kids love to exercise, some don't. If they love to exercise it will be easy for you to get them to go outside and spontaneously move their bodies. There is a fine balance between letting them determine what they want to do and directing them. The best is to try many activities and sports and see what they like the most. A child who learns how their body moves will build body awareness as well as self-awareness. Gymnastics, dance, yoga (see next section), and martial arts are particularly good for teaching body awareness. These skills can help them listen to their bodies, and in turn, help them avoid injuries in other sports and activities.

For kids who don't like to participate in sports, be creative in getting them to move. Dance around the house, chase them (in fun), play tag, be silly, jump on a trampoline (or bed ☺), do a quick clean-up game that includes running around. The younger you get them to move, the more inclined they are to continue as they get older, even into adulthood, which will prevent obesity and other serious health problems, now and in the future. Remember that *FUN* is the key word for encouraging kids to move their bodies!

Yoga

Some see yoga as a class of stretching. It is about stretching, but it's so much more. Yoga is also about mindfulness, breath control, body awareness, meditation, and it can also be very physically challenging, depending upon the class. Beyond the physical gains from yoga, there are many emotional benefits from it too. Yoga helps the body relax and move from a sympathetic state to a parasympathetic state, relieving stress and tension. The brain releases calming hormones instead of stress hormones, and it's an avenue for self-expression and awareness. Yoga also helps improve immune function and digestion.

I love yoga but I was resistant for years. My excuse was, "I can't do yoga, I am the most unlimber person in the world!" When I finally tried it, I realized that our bodies can become more limber with practice. It was hard at first but I started slow with a video in my basement and then moved to a class. Now I love it and can't go a week without it. Oh how I wish I would have done it with my kids when they were young! A neighbor recently told me that when he began doing yoga daily, within 10 months he'd lost 40 pounds, and was able to stop taking medication for both physical and emotional issues, saving him $700 per year.

Begin yoga wherever you feel comfortable. You can start by trying free videos on YouTube or picking some up from the library. When your kids see other kids doing yoga on the video, they will be more encouraged to do it themselves. Going to a class together will create experiences and memories you both will cherish.

Nutrition

Nutrition is complicated for many people. New diets and fads about what to eat and what not to eat constantly bombard us. Unless you spend a lot of time researching and studying nutrition, you're never quite sure what to do. However, it is important to note that *what we eat influences our physical and mental health*.

Scientists have discovered that there is a connection between the gut health and brain health. Meaning if there is an imbalance in the intestinal microflora (which includes a whole host of organisms, including friendly bacteria), then your personality can change, your energy can drop, your health can be challenged, and it can be the beginning of illness—physical and mental. Dr. Maya Shetreat-Klein, a pediatric neurologist and author of *The Dirt Cure*, writes that "food is constantly changing kids' bodies, brains, and even genes—for the better or for worse." Dr. Shetreat-Klein, along with many other doctors and researchers, believes that the food we eat is key to a healthy mind and body. I highly recommend her book!

5 IMPORTANT FACTS ABOUT NUTRITION TO HELP SUPPORT EMOTIONAL HEALTH

- Vitamin D3, fish oil, and a good probiotic are the most important supplements most everyone can take.
- Juicing (which is different from smoothies) is one of the best forms of supplemental nutrition.
- Sugar is more addictive than many drugs and alcohol.
- Eliminating high-allergen foods such as gluten, dairy, soy, corn, and eggs can help with many physical and emotional aliments from anxiety to autoimmune disorders.
- Eating healthy fats such as olive oil, nuts, avocados, and butter (yay!) are as important as eating proteins. Butter is actually important for a child's brain development!

This book cannot review all the research and data on nutrition, but please know this one fact: if your child is moody, reactive, hyper, depressed, tired, and or suffering from illness, it's important to consider that food may have something to do with it. The trick is to figure it out which foods are problematic and which ones aren't. You can determine if any foods are causing physical or mental issues by eliminating them for 2 weeks and then reintroducing them one at a time. Sadly, sugar, wheat, dairy, eggs, soy (it's in many processed foods), and corn (also in a lot of different foods) are the most common culprits. Sometimes kids are sensitive to more than one type of food. If you have any questions or concerns, consult your doctor, a nutritionist, a naturopath, or chiropractor with extra training in nutrition.

My niece has many food sensitivities—too long a list to name here. When she eats something she is sensitive to, her mood can change quickly. Then she goes into what I call a "grouchy hangover." She can become oversensitive, angry, judgmental, sad (even depressed), unable to think straight, and just plain crabby! This can last for 24 to 48 hours. Know that foods can affect moods—a lot.

Getting your kids to eat healthy is hard sometimes, especially if bad habits are in place. To get started, an 80/20 rule is good to follow. Eat healthy 80% of the time (lots of veggies and fruits, nuts, seeds, legumes, whole grains, unprocessed meat, whole-fat dairy products, and healthy fats and oils). As you and your children notice how much better you feel fueled by healthy food, you'll have an easier time ramping that up closer to 100%. For anyone's health and well-being, but especially for growing children, sugar can be a treat for special occasions, and avoid processed foods that contain chemical texturing agents, preservatives, flavoring and coloring additives, and trans fats (partially hydrogenated oils). For every dollar you spend on high-quality, nutrient-dense groceries, you'll likely save many dollars on medical and therapy bills. You'll also enjoy the benefits of fewer sick days, and happier, healthier kids. What a wise investment! Here are a few ways to encourage you and your kids to eat healthy:

- Set a good example; children learn by watching.
- Serve a nutritionally dense breakfast. Even if your child doesn't have an appetite early in the morning, you can offer smoothies, which can go down more easily, or put a nutrition bar in a pocket for later.
- Offer healthy choices by stocking your shelves with only healthy foods.
- Let them help you cook, create, and explore new foods.
- Have your kids help you plan meals or the week's menu. If they have a say, they'll be more invested in showing up and eating it.
- Create family traditions, such as "pizza night" or "foreign cuisine day."
- Raise awareness by teaching your kids how to read labels. Investigate the various ingredients and decide what's good and not so good for your brains and bodies.
- View healthy choices as "yummy" because they promote health, well-being, and make for a truly satisfying meal or snack.

- View unhealthy choices as rare exceptions because they aren't so good—and if you or your child are sensitive, they don't feel good either!
- Boost nutrition by adding some spinach, kale, a bit of cucumber, and/or avocado to their morning smoothie (they won't even know it's in there!).
- Use healthy dips, sauces, and dressings to add interesting flavors to foods.
- Pay attention to texture: some kids love crunchy, some love smooth, some love it all.
- View shopping and meal preparation as an important use of your time as it nurtures your bodies and promotes emotional well-being.
- Have fun, keep it positive, and create happy family times around food.

Play

Tea parties, card and board games, catch or tag football are common among some families, and unfortunately a lost art in others. The American Academy of Pediatrics promotes play as essential to a child's development, because research shows that it improves learning and cognitive, physical, social, and emotional well-being. Yet, play has been happening less and less in schools and schedules are getting so tight that play doesn't naturally fit into life. Fortunately, play is making a comeback because we now know it is critical to the healthy development of kids and teens. It teaches kids so much, including how to work with others, manage feelings, think, plan, make decisions, and read other people's emotions. Play also promotes self-expression, self-regulation, and healthy boundaries—basically emotional wellness.

Play can also be very therapeutic. Children struggling with difficult life experiences—stressful or traumatic—will benefit from play. Doing something completely different and getting away from a difficult situation gives a well-needed break. They may also process the scenario that's been difficult by acting it out in play. A friend who had a premature infant said her other girls often played "hospital," because having their sister there was so difficult for them. If your kids are stressed or acting out their trauma in play, don't try to fix it or guide it in a certain direction, let them play it out (as long as they are safe)—eventually they will master or resolve the issues they are working on. If you have concerns about them or what you see, talk to your pediatrician or consult a therapist. (See chapters 10 and 11).

Some parents don't really know how to play (I'm guilty of that—still working on it) so it can be hard to teach and encourage your child to play. But the cool thing is that children naturally know how to play, and you can follow their lead and have fun doing it! The first step is to find out what your child likes to do. This may change over time, so be flexible. Some kids might like cool science experiments, some only want to do something physical and outdoors, others may have music interests, want to cook with you, draw or create, build Legos or blocks, play with dolls or stuffed animals, tell jokes, play "I Spy"—the list is endless, but please note that video games are not on it. Instead provide the raw materials your child needs to pursue their interests, explore their imaginations, experience the world around them, or express their creativity. If you have multiple children, at times they may all want to do something different and you will be challenged by keeping multiple balls in the air. Try your best to give each child the attention they need, but things happen and life isn't always balanced. This provides good lessons in compromise, cooperation, and give-and-take. Some people know how to make anything a game, even eating, but if you're at a loss, just go online and make a list of fun, creative family games you'd like to try with your kids. Ask your friends and relatives about games they enjoy playing as a family, and you'll probably get some great ideas. The more you play with each other, the more connected you'll feel. And your children will learn to enjoy playing with their siblings and other kids, and in turn, learn a lot about life, fun, and spontaneity.

A sampling of popular games:
- Play card and board games like Old Maid, Bingo, or Monopoly.
- Chase bubbles.
- Have a picnic (indoors or out).
- Play hide-n-seek.
- Decorate cookies together.
- Guess the mystery food.
- Have a pillow fight.
- Cut snowflakes out of paper.
- "I see something in Grandma's grocery store and it starts with the letter ___."
- "I spy with my little eye, something that is (name a color). Guess what it is!"
- Play music, dance, and freeze—see how silly everyone looks!

Music and Dance

Music can change someone's mood in seconds. Play music in your home and car. Be silly and dance. Show your kids that life is meant to be crazy and fun sometimes. Of course, the choice of music is key. If you don't like their music, take turns—make it a game. Music and dance feed the soul and help to release stress, break down barriers—and dance is fun and good exercise too.

Less Screen Time

Many of us fear the negative impact of technology on our children and society. It's estimated that kids spend four to seven hours a day in front of a screen and as little as 30 minutes outside. The American Academy of Pediatrics recommends that kids ages 3 to 18 spend only two hours per day in front of a screen, kids less than 2 years old should not have any screen time.

In her book, *It's Complicated: The Social Lives of Networked Teens*, Danah Boyd has thoroughly researched the impact of technology on our kids. She writes that our kids use technology for socialization because of their busy lifestyles. Other options like hanging out at the mall or playing a pick-up game of baseball, are not as available as they used to be. I would add that much less time is being spent in nature, as free time or quality downtime. To offset their time with technology, give them lots of screen-free options such as spending face-to-face time with friends, playing sports, and other outdoor activities.

More Nature

Being outside is good for all of us. The condition "nature deficit disorder" has been identified, and it is becoming an epidemic. Every child is different, some love being outdoors and some prefer to be inside. But kids will go outside more if you are out there with them. Walking, playing with your pets, fun nature activities, or sports will encourage more outdoor time. Of course, playing with other kids outdoors offers even more benefits. A UCLA study of two groups of 6th graders at a camp showed that kids who had no electronic exposure for five days showed a significantly higher ability to determine emotions on the faces of subjects they were shown. Kids learn so much about life when they are playing with other kids and exploring the world outdoors.

Danielle Cohen of www.childmind.org writes that being outdoors builds confidence, promotes creativity and imagination, teaches responsibility, provides different stimulation, gets kids moving, makes them think, and reduces stress and fatigue. Research has shown that getting kids outside, moving, playing, and exploring will help them reset psychologically, so they are better able to cope with life.

Essential Oils

Herbs have been used to create natural scents and to facilitate healing for centuries. Fortunately, now they are easily available at your local health food stores or through a few different companies such as *Young Living* or *Doterra*. To use essential oils, you can get a diffuser to circulate a scent(s) in the air throughout a room or your entire home. Or you can apply the oil on your skin—the best places to apply them for quick results are under your toes, on the bottom of your feet, your neck or belly. Don't ingest them without talking to someone who specializes in the use of oils—they can harm you if used incorrectly. Begin slowly and if you aren't sure, find someone who is trained in Essential Oils or take a class about them. There are Facebook pages that focus on how to use oils for healing. Check with your doctor if you or your child have any specific health conditions (or you are pregnant) before using essential oils.

Here are a few essential oils that can help a variety of issues:

- *Lavender* calms the nervous system, lowers blood pressure and heart rate, helps with mild insomnia, helps decrease depression and anxiety.
- *Peppermint* is also calming and helps with stress.
- *Lemon* eases nervousness, stress, and insomnia.
- *Chamomile* helps with sleep, anxiety, and depression.
- *Eucalyptus* fights fatigue, anxiety, depression, stress, and is calming.
- *Ylang Ylang* is calming and relaxing. It delivers a feeling of self-love, confidence, joy, and peace.
- *Sandlewood* is often used to aid meditation and focus. It is calming.

Sleep

Kids need more sleep than adults to support their developing minds and bodies. Unfortunately, they typically do not get enough sleep. Life can be very demanding and tight schedules often do not allow enough time to wind down and relax before bed. It's recommended that school-age kids get 7 to 12 hours sleep and teens get 7 to 11 hours sleep. If school starts early, this can be hard to accomplish. Some kids are chronically tired but may not show it, because kids tend to keep going; they may even rev up when they are tired.

The sleep structure common today (sleeping for a long stretch at night) became popular during the industrial revolution so workers could get up early and get to their jobs. Our natural states, however, might require a different sleep schedule. Taking a daytime nap regularly might be helpful for many kids and adults, but with busy schedules, that can be hard to fit in. As an alternative, a technique called the Tahiti Pose can be very refreshing when you/they are tired. Lay on your back with your feet up on a chair at a 90-degree angle and your arms above your head or out to the side. Fifteen minutes like this is equivalent to one hour of sleep. The Tahiti Pose can also help us relax right before bedtime, as it helps the body move from an alert to a calm state, making it easier to fall asleep. It might be fun to do this with your kids (and your dogs and cats may love joining you too ☺).

As parents, we know when our kids are tired. We also know that getting a good night's sleep improves everyone's outlook on life. It can be hard to enforce more sleep with kids, but do your best to create a scenario where they will be able to—and even want to—go to bed and rest. Don't overschedule the evenings and weekends, discourage electronics 2 hours before bed (I know, easier said than done—even half an hour might help), make sure they have down time, spend time with them reading, storytelling, dreaming about life, and imagining new possibilities. Bedtime routines can be powerful inducers of sleep. The more positive they feel about bedtime and sleep, the more rest they will get and the happier they will be in life; and they will be able to handle drama, trauma, and stress much easier!

Tips for Teachers

The younger the body, the more important it is to be well rested and well fed, and to move, have fun, and be expressive, especially in a learning environment. If kids don't get to move, they will feel tired, trapped, bored, distracted, fidget, and quickly (and inaccurately) be labeled in some settings as misbehaving! Research shows that kids can only sit still and listen for as many minutes as they are old. So for a six-year-old, that's six minutes! When kids are stressed or traumatized their attention span can be even less, so keeping them engaged with movement is even more important. Unfortunately, long periods of sitting still and doing intellectual work is more common than not in an average school.

Cultivating a healthy culture in your classroom may expose some student's to healthy body choices for the first time. For others, you are continuing to foster healthy choices and may give them an opportunity to teach their peers. Spending time teaching healthy eating and lifestyle choices ensures you hit district, state, and federal health standards.

Use these tips to guide you on how to help your students learn and practice taking care of their bodies:

- Create a morning movement routine—this is a great place to incorporate yoga or another other fun movement activity you prefer. You can change the movement to match the day of the week. Check out www.gonoodle.com.
- Have learning stations where there is a different movement at each station. Standing up, sitting down, bouncy balls, fun chairs, stair steps.
- Allow for students to have opportunities to stand and move for a few minutes, at about every 10-15 minutes for K-2 and every 20-30 minutes for grades 3-5.
- Work in a variety of groups and let students sit on a variety of flexible seating options like exercise balls, wiggle stools, carpet remnants, or pillows.
- Bring in movement specialists, such as a yoga teacher, fitness instructor, or dance teacher, to expand student horizons and maybe tap into an unknown strength or interest.
- Take a Brain Break and throw a ball or balloon around; when they have the ball, they have to answer a question or have a new idea, or fact.
- When teaching about a foreign country or language, try doing the traditional dances of those people.
- Before showing them a dance from a different country have them free dance what they think it might be as you play the foreign music.
- Stand in a circle and everyone jump and make a funny face all at once.

- If a student is falling asleep in class or unable to attend, *let them sleep* (in the nurse's office or a safe supervised space away from peers is best).
- Diffuse or spray essential oils in your classroom. A mix of lavender and peppermint both calms the body while engaging the brain for alertness. There are oils to cleanse the air of germs, oils to engage the right or left hemispheres of the brain, oils to calm, and oils to focus. Test what your students like best.
- Model and encourage healthy eating when you can. Let them try unusual fruits and veggies or experiment with a fun and unique recipe (lots of recipes online under "fun healthy kids snacks").

8

Nurturing the Spirit

Imagine Story
by Calvin T. Hurd, age 28

Imagine...being a big brother to a 3-year-old.

Imagine...being 6 years old and having 21 bullets fired at you and your 3-year-old brother.

Imagine...your 3-year-old brother being shot right next to you.

Imagine...finding out you're going to be an only child.

Imagine...having to grow up fast.

Imagine...having to take care of your mom at age 7.

Imagine...being 14 and joining the very thing that killed your brother—a gang.

Imagine...being 17 and realizing you are worth more than what you've become.

*Imagine...*being baptized at the age of 21 and experiencing a renewal of life.

*Imagine...*being 25 and suffering a mental break down.

*Imagine...*being diagnosed with a mental illness.

*Imagine...*learning that childhood trauma has caught up with you.

*Imagine...*learning that 4 months of play therapy was not enough to deal with trauma.

*Imagine...*finding a therapist

*Imagine...*being heavily medicated to cope.

*Imagine...*being 27 and giving your life fully to Christ.

*Imagine...*creating coping skills through biblical scripture.

*Imagine...*reducing the medication.

*Imagine...*getting back to life with brand new coping skills and hope for new beginnings.

*Imagine...*being a business owner.

*Imagine...*finally being a survivor of childhood trauma.

~ひ~

Spirituality

Spirituality means connecting to the essence of your being, which is often referred to as the soul, spirit, or inner self. How you express your spirituality is unique for each one of us. Religion, prayer, meditation, quiet reflection, embracing a community, and finding purpose are a few ways to nurture spiritual well-being.

Embracing and exploring your spirituality promotes emotional wellness because contemplating greater meaning or higher purpose in life boosts your resilience when you are challenged by difficult life experiences.

Religion and Prayer

Religion is a practiced form of spirituality, such as Christianity, Judaism, Buddhism, Islam, or Hinduism. Religion brings a sense of tradition, community, and "guidelines" for life that can often help kids, teens, and adults who are struggling. Prayer is typically a part of religion, and research shows that religious people spend less time in the hospital, they tend to live longer, ward off cognitive decline, and have more years without disabling illnesses such as stroke, heart disease, and cancer. Research also shows prayer helps people with depression recover faster.

In her book, *Tears to Triumph (2016)*, Marianne Williamson writes, "Faith helps us during periods of depression and sadness because it gives us the patience to endure." Many mental health professionals believe that having a positive form of faith and spiritual awareness helps emotional difficulties heal more easily. Talking to your child about faith or spirituality is very important to their internal awareness. They will typically follow your belief systems, but as they mature, a wider circle of friends and resources may influence them. It's important to know that you can't force a religious or spiritual belief on anyone. It's a journey everyone needs to travel on his or her own. Helping your children gain awareness of their higher selves and find their own personal meaning will bring a more positive sense of self and purpose.

Tips for helping kids expand their spirituality, life purpose, and inner reflection:

- Talk to them about your beliefs and how they might differ from other religions/belief systems.

- Ask them what they think and believe.
- Read age-appropriate books that will trigger thoughts and ideas about the meaning of life.
- Be in nature as much as possible (nature promotes calm, internal reflection).
- Encourage awareness and compassion for those who might be less fortunate, such as people dealing with homelessness, poverty, or disability.
- Teach them about giving to others by donating your used goods, money, or time, such as volunteering for a community clean up, food bank, or soup kitchen. When they see you giving, they can be inspired to give as well. (For more on this, see "Finding Purpose by Helping Others" later in this chapter.)

Meditation

Meditation is the practice of quiet awareness, thought, and reflection. It brings us to a tranquil place which promotes a stronger connection to our spirituality. Mindfulness meditation is a conscious effort to keep bringing your wandering thoughts back to the present moment, which offers the mind a peaceful resting place. Praying can be a form of meditation, if your mind is peaceful and you feel a sense of contentment as you pray. Research has shown the benefits of meditation for adults, and remarkable benefits for kids.

THE BENEFITS OF MEDITATION FOR KIDS

- Reduced stress, hyperactivity, impulsiveness, and inattention
- Improved parent-child relationships
- Improved self-esteem
- Potentially decreased medication use
- Improved sleep

Getting your child to meditate may be tricky, depending upon their age. Younger kids want to do whatever you are doing, so modeling meditation or doing it with them will be key. Making it fun will be even better! If they are older and don't want your suggestions, you can simply offer them information, and talk about how much it's helping you. When they see the difference it makes in you, they may be more interested in it for themselves.

There are many forms of meditation for adults and kids. Search for information online and find meditations on YouTube. Deepak Chopra has a few fun and simple meditations for kids on his website www.chopra.com. Find a quiet place in your home to meditate regularly. Fill it with comforting items, soft pillows, and calming smells or candles, which can help settle your mind.

I've been practicing medication for years, and yet, I still have a hard time quieting my mind. It's easier if I listen to a guided meditation or music that is meditation-based. If you look online for "power up meditations," you will find a few very simple, short, powerful meditations to use when you wake up in the morning, and maybe late afternoon, when you could use a reboot for the evening chores, routines, and family interactions. If you are grounded and relaxed, your kids will be too.

Gratitude meditations are an easy start. Sit or lie in a comfortable position, in a quiet place (you can even do this while in your parked car). Put one or both hands on your heart. Begin by paying attention to your breathing. Let your breathing slow down and notice each breath as you breathe in and out. As you relax, name at least three things you are grateful for. If you can name more, that's great—the more the better. You can do this anytime during the day, but opening and ending your day with a gratitude meditation helps change brain patterns to become more positive, which helps you to handle stress more easily.

A meditation practice evolves over time. It's like a muscle you work to strengthen. The more you use it, the stronger it gets. Showing your kids how to meditate will be life changing for them (and you). It takes time and commitment, but it's well worth it.

I LOVE YOU MEDITATION

A great meditation for you to connect with your kids is something I call the "I Love You Meditation." I often suggested this to parents of preemies in the hospital when they had to go home and couldn't be with their sick babies. Find a quiet place to sit or lay down. You can also do this as you wake up in the morning or while drifting off to sleep at night. Hold one hand over your heart and begin by noticing your breathing. As you follow your breathing, think of your child as an infant, in that precious stage as a newborn. Imagine your child as an infant lying on your chest, sleeping peacefully as they once did. As you imagine them resting, surround them with the love you felt for them, then and now—just pure love. Imagine them feeling it—no matter how many miles away they are. The bond between a parent and child is strong—if they are struggling or your relationship is going through challenges, this meditation can help ground you, so you can stay lovingly connected to them. Try it and see how it feels.

Community

Remember the saying, "It takes a village to raise a child"? Well it's so true. Raising and teaching children about life takes place not only at home, but in neighborhoods, groups, teams, and community settings. Communities are changing and, sadly, even breaking apart. Back in the day, neighborhoods were where kids spontaneously gathered with other kids to play outside, run around, and play pick-up games. Nowadays, this has has shifted to scheduled playdates, organized sports, and online games.

Being surrounded by a community teaches a child important life lessons about getting along and compromising, about their place in the world, about "playing" different roles in different settings, and about a sense of belonging. Communities also give kids (and adults) a place to lean on when they need help. Research has shown that neighborhoods and communities that encourage togetherness are even safer than those who don't. Research also shows that face-to-face interaction is invaluable for building relationships, warding off depression, and feeling connected to others. Screen time cannot replace actual face time for boosting emotional wellness. I can't stress enough how important it is to get a child involved in whatever community they feel comfortable in—and to give them opportunities to expand their horizons, explore other options, and stretch their comfort zone.

In this electronic, highly-scheduled world, how do you create more community opportunities for your kids? Here are a few ideas:

- Get to know your neighbors. Have a block party, backyard get-togethers, or create fun events in the neighborhood like having a giant garage sale, a progressive dinner, or a bake off.
- Find some older neighbors and offer to help with yard work or things around their homes.
- Create community or neighborhood game nights or movie nights.
- Go to a local park and encourage the kids to play informal recreational sports like kickball, disc golf, or just a simple game of tag.
- Go to a neighborhood food bank or community service and offer to help.
- Ask kids over to your house—have/bake cookies and they will come!
- Get your kids involved in a local organized sports

team or a club aligned with their interests.
- Create a simple play (theater type) that kids can participate in.
- Volunteer with them at a local organization they are interested in.

Finding Purpose by Helping Others

As kids grow and seek to understand themselves and find their identity, they also embark on a journey to find purpose in their lives. Finding purpose isn't something anyone can do for anyone else, but we can give kids opportunities and experiences that help shape how they feel about themselves and the world. Carey Wallace (Nov 10, 2015, *Time*) suggests that we begin by asking our children what they think their best qualities and strengths are, what their best relationships have been, whether they've ever helped someone, and how it felt to be appreciated. These conversations give kids validation for positive qualities. When they do things to help you or others, show them how much it meant to you and ask them how it felt to give.

Offer kids opportunities to give back, to help out someone else, or to work physically hard on a project for someone else. (I may be old-fashioned but I believe hard physical labor, such as moving, painting, gardening, or cleaning up, is good for the soul.) They can see their results quickly, making these accomplishments gratifying. Mixing with and helping others is a way for kids to get exposure to other lifestyles and the needs connected with them. Walking up to someone new or helping someone you once feared or judged will give you a new perspective about life. Starting when children are young will create caring, thoughtful citizens. Here are some suggestions:

- Find a few different organizations that help the less privileged and bring your children to help. Let them decide where they like working the most, and then return repeatedly.
- Take them to art or history museums to see how others have lived in different times and different places.
- Watch documentaries about the lives of others in different parts of the world.
- Travel to other regions, or even to another part of your local area, where the lives of people are very different from your own.
- Expose them to social change projects they may find interesting.

Tips for Teachers

Encouraging students' to share their beliefs and honoring their belief systems is another way to build a sense of community in your classroom. We all desire to be valued as humans. Because spirituality is so deeply rooted in many of us, making space for sharing and accepting each others' beliefs allows your students to feel safe, connected, valued, and hopeful. Talking about greater meaning, purpose in life, priorities, and intention is a way to cultivate reflection, explore values, and inspire kids to set goals.

In the fast-paced, hyper-connected classroom, a few minutes of meditation can make a world of difference to a child's ability to focus, learn, and cope with stress.

Research studies and schools that have started a "quiet time" and/or meditation practices have shown an increase in the retention of information, decrease in truancy, decreased stress and depression, and greater self-esteem in students. Honoring each other, helping students find purpose and motivation, and cultivating peaceful calm in the classroom are all critical components to a solid foundation upon which academics and character traits can be built and strengthened. Try these tips to help you in these areas:

- Make a time and space for students to share and ask questions of one another about their beliefs, values, priorities, and goals.
- Invite families and students to share traditions and history during special holidays (refer to your school district's policies on diversity, holidays, religion, beliefs, tolerance, and equity).
- Have each student create a "culture box," and then share and answer questions about their own culture. Their box can showcase symbolic items and pictures of the things each child believes in, values, hopes for, and *Imagines* in life. (Give time and resources within the school day to accommodate students who aren't able to complete this at home.)
- Encourage students to use positive language and tolerance when sharing differing viewpoints or personal beliefs. For example, "Thank you for sharing your insights, and *(not "but")* here is what I think." Or "That sounds really interesting. Here is what I believe."

- Find a meditation practice that works for your classroom. Go to www.calm.com or www.smilingmind.com.au, for free meditation practices to get you started.
- Use *My Imagine Journal*™ to encourage students to write down what they see as their purpose in life, both for themselves, their communities, and globally.
- Help your students develop and discover how they can make their *Imagines* and intentions come to fruition.

PART FOUR

When You Need Extra Help

AS PARENTS, TEACHERS, AND YOUTH LEADERS we can do everything we know to try and help a child, and yet, they may still struggle. Sometimes kids are just complicated or impacted more than we realize and we can't make sense of it or find a way to help them. This section will suggest steps to take when nothing you do seems to be working, and offer tips to help you take care of yourself in the process of caring for your children or your students.

9

Taking Care of Yourself Too

Imagine Story
by Alana Weaver, mom to Makayla

Imagine...being blindsided by a diagnosis for your child that would change everything.

Imagine...trying to explain a disease to your 9-year-old that neither you nor the doctors fully understand.

Imagine...knowing that how you react, your ability to cope will set the tone for your child's willingness to fight and stay alive.

Imagine...days and nights filled with crippling fear, pain, and uncertainty.

Imagine...holding your child tightly, tears streaming down both your faces, as you plead with God to let you trade places with them.

Imagine... doctor after doctor, surgery after surgery, medication after medication. All of minimal help and far from a much-needed cure.

Imagine... rearranging your entire life to accommodate a disease—giving up your job, your time, your sleep, yourself. All to no avail and at a high personal cost.

Imagine... feeling like you failed at the most important job you ever had—protecting and taking care of your baby.

Imagine... a guilt of such great portions that it consumes every part of your own body and life, similar to the very disease you are trying to help your child fight.

Imagine... with a trembling heart, making the decision to turn darkness into light. Tragedy into triumph. Loneliness into words of hope.

Imagine... knowing that although it is not up to you how the story ends, it is however, up to you how you live it.

Imagine... truly living everyday as if it were the last. Celebrating every victory of your child, major and minor, as if it were the best victory ever.

Imagine... knowing that although love can't fix all things, it can heal them; making them bearable to face and giving a purpose to the greatest heartbreak you've ever known.

Imagine... finding more than you lost through facing an incurable disease.

Imagine... making the choice every day, no matter how hard or painful, to build a legacy greater than any life you could've ever crafted.

*Imagine…*learning that the only way you can ever take care of anyone, the only way you can ever be of any good to the world around you, is to first take care of yourself the best way you know how—spiritually, physically, and emotionally.

PARENTS, TEACHERS, COUNSELORS, CLINICIANS, humanitarians—we all have something in common: we love to help and take care of others—so much so that we often forget to take care of ourselves. *If we are depleted, we cannot adequately give to others.* If your bucket is empty, there is nothing left to share. So, before you begin nurturing your children, students, or others, take the time to nurture yourself.

How Tired Are You?

Check in with yourself. Are there times you feel like you could stop and sleep for a day, a week, a month? Are you having mental or physical symptoms that you don't understand (i.e. irritability, depression, headaches, stomach aches, or rashes)? Do you feel like you are on a treadmill that just won't turn off? Do you sometimes just want to scream, run, hide, or do something destructive that you would regret forever? If any of these symptoms are true for you—even just slightly so—it's time to ramp up taking care of yourself.

I remember going to see a doctor I greatly respected because I was so tired all the time. He said, "You have what I call, *The Mom Syndrome.* You overdid it, taking care of everyone else and now you have adrenal exhaustion." Yes, many of us forget to take care of ourselves while we are taking care of others. We put "me" on the back burner for so long, the burner barely lights. We may be givers—those who love to give to others—but, it doesn't serve *us*, and eventually it doesn't serve those we are taking care of. Did you know that:

- 43% of all adults suffer adverse health effects from stress.
- 75-90% of all doctor's office visits are for stress-related ailments and complaints.
- According to WebMD.com, the lifetime prevalence of an emotional disorder in more than 50% of cases is due to chronic, untreated stress.
- Caregivers often predecease the disabled or sick adult they are caring for.

Remember if you push it down, it comes out sideways—eventually. In other words, if you don't process painful emotion, like anger, resentment, sadness, or worry, it will create painful results, such as angry outbursts, depression, and physical ailments. It *will* happen if you don't manage your stress. I understand how hard it is to make time for yourself when your day is already full and it seems like there is not enough time to add one more thing. But it's time—time to do something different—time to take care of you, too. In fact, by taking care of yourself, you actually become more efficient and more effective, therefore creating more time in your life for what's important, including taking care of yourself as well as you take care of others.

What holds many people back from self-care is feelings of guilt and worries about being selfish. But what if you changed your mindset? Who would you be with this thought: "I need to make time for myself every day—blocks of at least 15 or 20 minutes just for me." And: "I am important enough to take time for me, every day." And: "To be of service to others, I must first be of service to myself, because when I'm running on empty, I'm of service to no one." You might not believe it at first, but after a while, you will see a difference in how you feel and how you interact with life. Wouldn't it be nice to enjoy and be present each day? To smile with your family? To have the energy to play and love life?

In fact, self-care is something you can tend to every minute of every day, as you weigh what is best for you in each moment and find the right balance. Sometimes you decide to give outwardly, and sometimes you decide to give inwardly.

When we are a caregiver for a loved one who needs intensive attention and care, life can get particularly overwhelming. Whether they are physically sick or emotionally challenged, they require an extra time and extra effort. As a parent and/or a caretaker, it can feel as if our lives are being swept away. Emotions like anger, resentment, guilt, worry, even defensiveness can permeate our relationships and wear us down. Our bodies, our minds, and even our spirits become depleted and we don't have much left to give. If this is the case, it's even more critical for you to have a plan for filling up your own bucket—finding space in your day just for you. It doesn't have to be much, but it has to be something.

I'm challenging you today to begin to improve the habit of taking care of yourself! Begin by writing notes to yourself and put them on your mirror, computer, refrigerator, dashboard, or phone, telling yourself: "I am worth it!" Or: "Do something nice for yourself today!" And: "You deserve time for yourself!" These encouraging reminders can help you create new habits.

It takes 21 days to create or change a habit. Make a plan. Write down 21 things you can do for yourself each day. Write what you love to do—small things and big things. What nurtures you? Do the small things on busy days, bigger things on lighter days. Make a commitment to yourself, and know that in turn, you are making a commitment to those you love because you will be physically and mentally healthier—more balanced and less strung out, capable of taking better care of others and accomplishing your dreams and desires. If you don't do it now, you will regret it in one, five, or ten years when you're tired and your health is challenged; you will look back and wish you did.

Here are some suggestions to include in your plan for taking care of yourself. All of these nurture the brain/mind, body, and spirit; choose the ones that fit for you.

1. Sit quietly for 15-20 minutes, perhaps daydreaming or looking out the window (consider doing this if you commute by public transportation!)
2. Spend time reading a book or your favorite magazine.
3. Spend time among plants—indoors or outdoors.
4. Go for a walk, run, or bike ride.
5. Exercise—work out or play a sport.

6. Write a list of affirmations for yourself.
7. Write an *Imagine* story (see chapter 5).
8. Take a nap.
9. Carve out alone time, where you can do whatever pleases you in the moment.
10. Explore your neighborhood or town.
11. Challenge yourself to hug ten people in one day.
12. Spend time with an animal—petting, cuddling, play with, or watching.
13. Sing.
14. Dance.
15. Watch a light-hearted or funny movie.
16. Watch inspiring videos online.
17. Pick some flowers, or if you can, buy yourself some flowers.
18. Get a massage.
19. Pamper yourself (get a pedicure, a haircut, a facial).
20. Meditate.
21. Do yoga.
22. Color, paint, or do anything creative.
23. Find a community to spend time in, without your kids ☺ (neighbors, friends, card players, book clubs).
24. Practice smiling—making your facial muscles form a smile produces feel-good brain chemistry.
25. Play The Gratitude Game (see chapter 6).
26. Write your *Imagine* dreams and aspirations for the future, near and far!

And the list goes on. Review chapters 6, 7, and 8 for more ideas on nurturing yourself.

Once you've done something for yourself every day for 21 days, ask yourself, "How do I feel?" "Do I feel more grounded, energetic, balanced?" Then, don't stop with 21 days—keep going and make this a lifetime commitment. If you do, you're more likely to live a longer, healthier life. Your brain and body need time to rest; they weren't built to withstand constant pressure—they were built to require respite in order to enjoy and love life. Who would you be with this thought: "I deserve to live a life of joy!"

Tips for Teachers

It wasn't until I began working more closely with teachers that I realized, you guys are stressed! (As a parent, I never got that impression.) Overworked, underpaid, micromanaged, no time—the list is very long. Reading the *Teacher Imagine Stories* later in this book will make anyone realize what hard-working, dedicated people teachers are. Yet, the body, mind, and spirit can only do and take so much. Much of what is written above applies to teachers, but here are a few more specific tips for self-care so you can remain shaping, changing, and loving your precious students.

- Laugh with your students.
- Go to www.gonoodle.com and dance/move with your students.
- Decorate your room with bright, happy posters and decor. Use warm colors, diffuse essential oils, bring in flowers.
- Include nature in your classroom, such as by

having live plants, a fish, nature posters, an herb garden, unobstructed windows to let in natural light.

- Play The Gratitude Game with your students (see chapter 6).
- Walk, meditate, or do yoga on a break.
- Take short (even 30 seconds) meditative breathing breaks throughout the day.
- Create healthy boundaries for yourself. This means knowing when to say "no" to whatever adds stress to your life. If it's essential then do it; if it's not, consider saying, "No!"
- Have an accountability partner to help you keep your boundaries. Check in with them each day or even each week to make sure you're both avoiding the road to Too Much!
- Eat nutritious foods. Bring healthy snacks everywhere you go to keep up your energy (and metabolism).
- Create a group of teachers and set aside time to socialize and talk about topics other than school.

10

TRADITIONAL THERAPIES AND THERAPISTS

IMAGINE STORY
by Makayla Grace, age 13

Imagine...finding out you have a brain disease.

Imagine...finding out it has no cure.

Imagine...only being nine years old.

Imagine...your whole life changing.

Imagine...being angry but not knowing who to be angry at.

Imagine...just wanting people to treat you like you're normal again.

Imagine...going through 20+ brain surgeries.

Imagine...knowing you could die every time you go back for one.

Imagine...wanting to die.

Imagine...realizing God has a plan for you.

Imagine...that plan being bigger than you could have ever dreamed possible.

Imagine...knowing that you can choose Joy and Strength over Sadness and Fear, no matter how you might feel.

Imagine...knowing that your illness has a purpose.

Imagine...knowing that you have a purpose.

Imagine...knowing that you were given the ability to change the lives around you by your Bravery.

Imagine...not letting your diagnosis win.

SOMETIMES YOUR CHILD (OR YOU) WILL NEED outside help to cope with extreme stress, difficult behaviors or patterns, or unresolved trauma. When your child needs help and your instinct tells you to use a more traditional approach, figuring out where to go first can be overwhelming. Here's some information about different types of mainstream doctors, therapists, and therapies. For information on less traditional, "complementary" therapies, see chapter 11.

Types of Therapists

Psychiatrist: A psychiatrist is a medical doctor who has completed medical school and a residency in psychiatry, and specializes in mental health. He or she focuses on the diagnosis, treatment, and prevention of mental, emotional, and behavioral disorders. A psychiatrist will most often do testing (primarily verbal and visual) to see if emotional imbalances and behaviors fit a psychological diagnosis based on the criteria of a medical guidebook called "the DSM-5" (*Diagnostic and Statistical Manual of Mental Disorders, 5th Edition*). Once a diagnosis has been made, he or she will recommend a course of treatment, which may include therapies and/or medications. Some psychiatrists offer psychotherapy themselves, such as talk therapy or cognitive behavioral therapy (see below), but many only offer diagnosis and medication management.

Clinical Psychologist: A clinical psychologist is an expert in mental health who, like a psychiatrist, has a doctoral degree and can be licensed to diagnose and treat mental, emotional, and behavioral disorders. But whereas a psychiatrist has a medical degree (MD) and can prescribe medication, a clinical psychologist has a PhD or PsyD, and cannot prescribe medication, but is specially trained in various forms of therapy. Many clinical psychologists will tailor treatment to the individual client's needs, using a variety of techniques, including talk therapy, cognitive behavioral therapy, somatic therapy, and EMDR. Some specialize in treating kids, teens, families, couples, and/or individuals.

Psychiatric Clinical Nurse Specialist (CNS) or Nurse Practitioner (NP): Both a clinical nurse specialist and a nurse practitioner in psychiatric/mental health have advanced training (a master's degree) in mental health. Both can diagnose and treat individuals and families; some specialize in kids and teens. Many use talk therapy or cognitive-behavioral therapy. The difference is that the NP can prescribe medications (under the supervision of a psychiatrist), while the CNS cannot.

Licensed Clinical Social Worker (LCSW): Social work is a psychology-related field designed to help individuals, families, and groups of people cope with life problems. An LCSW has a master's degree. Some work directly with individuals or groups, kids or adults, to help them cope or solve life problems in a group or individual setting. Others diagnose and treat mental, emotional, and behavioral issues using a variety of psychotherapy techniques. They cannot prescribe medication.

Counselor or Therapist (LPC): Most licensed professional counselors (LPC) call themselves "therapists". They typically have a master's degree in counseling and have to take a board exam in each state to receive a license. A therapist can assess, diagnose, and treat different emotional issues. They often use talk or cognitive behavioral therapies, but they may also use a variety of other therapeutic techniques. Some work with kids, some do not. They cannot prescribe medications.

All of the above professionals are typically recognized by insurance companies who reimburse for mental health. They all will be licensed by the state they work in and are overseen by a governing organization.

Life Coach: A life coach is someone who counsels individuals about personal challenges. They are not trained in mental health specifically, but they are trained in empowering their clients and helping them finding and following a direction in life. There are a variety of training programs for life coaches, but the right coach can help your child learn to make effective and balanced life choices. Life coaches are best used when there is no emotional imbalance, but a lack of purpose and direction in life. A life coach helps individuals determine their own options to consider, decide what they would prefer to do, and then build structures to attain their goals. Life coaches typically are not covered by insurance.

Types of Therapies

The types of therapies used by different therapists vary according to their training and the issues a child or teen might face. Beyond diagnosis, the goal of almost all therapy is to help someone become aware of their thinking, process emotion, be mindful of their interactions with others, cope with stress, change defeating behavior, improve communication skills, find better coping strategies, process difficult past experiences, release the stress and/or trauma of past or present events, and create a positive vision of life. Not all therapies are equally successful with each of these issues; some focus more on trauma processing, some help most with relationships, and some help more with self-reflection. There are many types of therapies, here are the more common ones.

Psychotherapy (Talk therapy): In psychotherapy, the therapist will talk with the child or teen to help them understand the unconscious meanings and motivations for their feelings and actions. The therapist will ask questions and reflect back what the client is saying. Talk therapy, especially with kids, requires a very safe, loving therapist. Healing using talk therapy is helpful, but somewhat limiting depending upon the child's problem. Younger kids are harder to talk with, simply because of their age and development. Talk therapy is good for helping someone understand what is happening in their world and why, but as research shows, it's difficult to achieve complete healing when there is trauma involved, for which brain-based treatments are more effective (see EMDR in this chapter, and EFT in chapter 11).

Cognitive Behavioral Therapy (CBT): There are many types of cognitive behavioral therapy. Its basic premise is that our thoughts—not the people or events around us—cause our feelings and behaviors. So if we change the way we think, we change the way we behave and feel. As with any therapy, the more positive and trusting the relationship is between the client and therapist, the more effective and quicker the results. CBT can be used with most children, young or old. It helps them break a cycle of thought and brings awareness to current thoughts tied to behaviors. Research has shown that CBT is effective with anxiety and depression. With trauma, it would be best to include other therapies that are more effective for trauma processing.

EMDR (Eye Movement Desensitization and Reprocessing): EMDR has been well-researched and is typically used in the treatment of trauma and/or extremely disturbing life experiences. Research shows that EMDR is even more effective than trauma-focused cognitive behavioral therapy, as it triggers the brain to properly process the traumatic memory, which markedly reduces or eliminates the emotional load. The central part of the technique is rapid eye movement while tracking a therapist's hand or light array as it moves quickly back and forth across the field of vision. Other stimulation can be used, such as tapping. It's a very effective treatment for children with trauma, and associated anxiety, attachment, anger, depression, nightmares, guilt, and self-esteem issues. You do need a skilled therapist for EMDR to be successful, so be diligent about researching the therapist's training and knowledge about using EMDR with kids. Ask if they use any other techniques as well. Sometimes therapies are combined together for an even better result. For more information and to find a clinician who does EMDR, go to www.emdr.com.

Play Therapy: Play therapy can be used for all ages, but it's particularly effective for young children. It's a form of therapy that uses play to allow children to communicate their inner emotions and experiences. Many (but not all) play therapists believe that children know the direction they need for expression and healing, so the therapist allows the child to direct the play without interference (also called child-centered play therapy). Play therapy is meant to be fun and loving, and it can be an important part of processing a stressful experience, especially for a young child.

Hypnotherapy: When most people think of hypnosis, they think of someone on stage in a trance, doing something funny or awkward. This is not the same as using hypnosis as a therapeutic treatment for emotional imbalances. Most hypnotherapists speak to their clients using a soft, kind voice to help relax into a state of consciousness where you can more easily process difficult life issues. You are still aware of your surroundings, but you are very relaxed. The analytical side of the brain is turned down very low or even off, and the emotional processing side of the brain is made more alert. In this state, guided by a good hypnotherapist, you can acknowledge and move through difficult emotions and experiences. I love hypnosis and have found it very helpful, particularly in times when I'm very stressed and/or processing a challenging time in my past. Be sure to find a licensed hypnotherapist. For trauma, make sure the practitioner also has psychotherapy training in trauma. Hypnotherapy can be a very effective, deep form of healing.

Art Therapy: Art therapy uses creative expression to allow children (of any age) to express their inner thoughts, feelings, and state of mind. Opening up creative channels helps anyone feel and express more. Art therapy can come in many forms—drawing, playing with sand, collage, sculpture, digital art, photography, and more. Find a therapist who is experienced and has a variety of techniques up his/her sleeve!

Body-Centered (also called Somatic) Psychotherapy: Body-centered or somatic psychotherapies include techniques where the body is included in the psychotherapy treatment. There are many forms of these therapies such as dance movement therapy, Hakomi, core energetics, and more. (Play therapy is considered body-centered therapy by some.) These therapies are not always considered mainstream therapies, but they are becoming more widely accepted, and they work very well for treating stress and trauma.

Somatic therapy postulates that by paying attention to sensations in the body, the client can move through deep emotional issues more quickly. Your body stores old emotions and traumatic experiences. When you listen to your body, using different techniques, you can release those emotions more effectively, and often much faster.

Depending upon the therapy, the child or teen will either be in a chair, lying on a massage table, playing, or dancing during therapy.

I recommend you carefully research each person in your area who does the work you feel will be the most helpful. Some will even work via Skype or over the phone. Be sure they are well-trained and get recommendations from your other trusted practitioners, Internet research, and/or from previous clients of theirs. A therapy may be the right type, but you might be seeing the wrong practitioner. Likewise, you may have found a wonderful therapist, but need a different type of therapy. Make sure a therapist has a sufficient level of experience—a minimum of two years—working with kids and teens, and a non-judgmental demeanor so your child will feel comfortable and accepted. You might visit the therapist first yourself and use your instincts, or take your child along and see how they do together. For therapy to work, your child must like and trust the therapist.

11

COMPLEMENTARY THERAPIES

IMAGINE STORY
by Aaron, age 8

Imagine...hearing your parents fight a lot, wishing they would stop.

Imagine...worrying about your mom because she cries a lot when they fight.

Imagine...your parents telling you they are not going to be married anymore.

Imagine...your parents still living together, being confused, wondering if they will get back together.

Imagine...selling your house and having to move around a lot.

Imagine...moving into your grandmother's house.

Imagine...your parents getting along better now than when they were married.

Imagine...spending time with both your mom and your dad in their respective homes.

Imagine...knowing one day you, your mom, and your brother will have your home together again.

～♫

ALTERNATIVE OR COMPLEMENTARY THERAPIES are healing modalities that are not always recognized by Western medical doctors or insurance companies. They may not be as "regulated" by the government. Some have been extensively researched, some have not. There are many types of complementary therapies, far more than can be listed here. Although I am a trained nurse of Western medicine, I have also trained in, experienced, and done extensive research about many types of complementary therapies. If it looks to me like it might work, I research it and try it. Here are ten different therapies I believe are very worthwhile to consider using with your kids and yourself for behavioral, emotional, psychological, even physical issues. My favorites for all ages are Emotional Freedom Technique (EFT), Homeopathy, and Neuro Emotional Technique (NET). Acupuncture is also good for older kids and adults. I'm sure there are many other very good therapies I haven't touched on here and some that really aren't worth your time or money. Be sure to try them yourself before you have your kids participate—and make sure the therapist is experienced.

Types of Therapies

Emotional Freedom Technique (EFT, also called Tapping): EFT is a form of energy psychology that combines the mind, the body, and its energy field to treat emotional and physical illness. Research has shown that EFT effectively treats anxiety, depression, addiction, symptoms of trauma, and a host of other emotional and physical problems. Although I have tried many forms of energy psychology techniques, EFT is my favorite.

EFT is based on the Chinese theory of energetic meridians. Chinese medicine believes that we all have meridians, which are energetic pathways that run through our bodies. When we are sick, those meridians are blocked. To heal, needles are placed in specific acupuncture points on the body to unblock the energy to restore health. Tapping also uses energetic meridians, except tapping with your fingers is done on the specific energy points instead of using needles.

Tapping is simple, easy, and effective. Research has shown that it can actually improve brain structure and function. It can be used for a wide range of emotional and physical issues from insomnia to headaches, anxiety, depression, and trauma. There are numerous tapping videos on YouTube and books that have been written even for kids (see the Reference section). You can teach yourself using these resources; there may even be DVDs at your local library. If significant trauma is the issue, it's best to be treated by a skilled therapist, but you can use tapping to treat some symptoms that might show up between sessions. Here is a quick overview you can try if you'd like.

How to use EFT/Tapping:

1. First help your child figure out the strongest negative emotion they are feeling at that moment, i.e. anger, sadness, or fear. Let them say it in their own words and tap with them, using their words.

2. Ask them how bad their emotion is before you begin, using a scale of 1-10, 10 being very bad and 1 being minimal. When you are done you can ask them again; hopefully it will be only at a 0 or 1 when you are done.

3. Ask them if they can tell where they are storing that emotion in their body—they might feel an ache in their belly, tightness in their neck or chest, a headache, or other pain (they may not be able to answer this question which is fine).

4. Tell them to do what you do and say what you say. (Note, every practitioner adapts their own version of the tapping sequence, if you see something you like better on YouTube go ahead and use it.)

5. Begin by using two fingers from either hand and tap with medium pressure just above your eyebrow to the inside, closer to your nose. Keep tapping as you say, "Even though I feel angry (or whatever emotion they named), I deeply and completely accept myself."

6. Now tap on your temple near your eye and say it again, "Even though I feel angry, I deeply and completely accept myself."

7. Now tap under your eye and say it again, "Even though I feel angry, I deeply and completely accept myself." (Continue to have your child follow your tapping and say what you say.)

8. Now move to under your nose, tapping and saying, "I'm so angry." Show a little emotion so your child can copy you.

9. Move to under your bottom lip and repeat. You can mix it up and say what your child might be angry at, perhaps school, friends, or confrontations: "I'm so angry that boy did that to me!"

10. Now tap just under the middle of your collar bone (either side of your chest—you can even switch sides of your body and face—it doesn't matter). Keep making statements that you think your child might feel. "So and so was so mean", "I am so mad at him!" Ask your child what they want to say and keep tapping.

11. Move to under your armpit about two inches down, keep making statements and tapping. Think about what your child might be feeling and make those statements or let them talk. Keep having them repeat after you.

12. Now move to the crevice or indentation on the top, pinky side of your hand and tap there while saying a profound statement about the emotion your child is feeling. "I am really mad!" Stay tapping on that spot on the hand and look up with your eyes, then down. Look to the left and then right (do not move your head, just your eyes), make a circle with your eyes, go back the other way, count to five out loud, hum a few notes and then count to five again. This is a critical part of the process, because it triggers different parts of the brain where emotion is often released. If your child is feeling

more emotional at this point, have them repeat all of the eye movements, humming and counting again a few times, all while tapping on the hand. Do it with them!

13. Now start all over again on the face and continue on all the spots you did the first round (eyebrow, temple, under your eye, under your nose, dimple in your chin, collar bone, below your arm pit, and the pinky side of the hand). Continue with this pattern until you can tell they are feeling better. This might take 5 minutes, or it might take 20 minutes (occasionally longer). They might sigh, take a deep breath, get distracted, smile. You can stop and ask them to give you a number between 1 and 10 naming how emotional they feel now. Hopefully, it will be much lower, even 0! If not, keep going or switch to another emotion—there is often more than one emotion to deal with at a time.

14. If they become really emotional during this process, don't stop, keep going. Tell them it will only last for a minute. If they need it, you can always tap on their bodies for them. Talking and tapping for them works, but it is better to let them participate. With little ones, under about 6 years old, you can tap back and forth on their legs or shoulders and just talk to them about something that is bothering them, it typically helps. You can even try it with babies!

15. One last note. Throughout the process, remind your child to think about the area on their bodies where they are holding the negative emotion (you asked them about this earlier)—it will help them to release the energy/emotion and keep them from feeling too emotional by focusing on their body not their emotions. Keeping them thinking about their bodies helps keep them grounded as well. It might sound complicated, but it's not. Practice it a few times and you will be able to use it anytime, anywhere. It's a great tool for many different issues!

A shortened version of EFT is simple yet it's still effective. It's what I use in the classroom, or on myself when I don't want anyone to know I'm tapping. Have kids cross their arms over their hearts and tap back and forth gently on the front of their shoulders, not too hard and not too soft. They can also cross their arms and tap under their arms, or just back and forth on their legs. If a child is upset, you can also tap on them, for them. It's most beneficial to tap this way for six to seven minutes, until you see them relax and they can refocus on what they are doing.

Finding an EFT therapist should not be too difficult. Look in the Reference section for recommended websites. Be sure to ask the therapist how long they have been practicing EFT and their experience with kids. If you want to use EFT for more serious issues such as trauma or depression, make sure they have experience working in those areas as well.

Classical Homeopathy: Classical homeopathy is a different form of medicine. Most medical doctors will not know about it or appreciate it, but I love homeopathy and honestly, I'm not sure I would still be alive if I hadn't used it for the last 20 years. Homeopathy is both an art (because it requires a different type of listening to the body) and a science. Homeopaths believe that all physical and emotional symptoms are signs that the body is out of balance, and the body can be strengthened to heal and rebalance itself.

Each patient is given a natural "remedy" that will support the body's constitution and ability to heal. Remedies are tiny pills or liquids that basically taste like water with a little flavoring. They are taken anywhere from every day to once a month or in even less-frequent intervals. Healing may be fast or slow, depending on how chronic the issues have become. It's a very individualized form of treatment. I was sold on homeopathy when a boy in my daughter's kindergarten class had serious chronic ear infections and was treated in the hospital with continuous weekly IV antibiotics for years (yes, years). The boy's mom decided to try homeopathy and he never had another ear infection again and no more antibiotics! Since then, I have referred hundreds of people to homeopaths. I've seen homeopathy help with anything from anxiety, fears, depression, Attention Deficit Disorder, to physical problems such as headaches, hormonal imbalances, food allergies, hyper and hypothyroidism. It helps a wide range of issues. Healing does take time, because it's strengthening the body's constitution so it can heal itself.

Finding the right homeopath is key. As always, make sure the homeopath has experience and good people skills. I recommend using a trained and certified classical homeopath, but some very good naturopaths and MD's practice classical homeopathy as well. Classical homeopathy is finding one remedy, not a mixture, that fits a specific client. The mixture other practitioners use can work for symptoms, but not the deeper healing a classical homeopath will pursue. See the Reference section for more information on homeopaths. Most insurance companies do not cover homeopathy, but it's not as expensive as other forms of treatment.

Neuro Emotional Technique (NET): I love energy releasing techniques. All stressful and emotionally impacting experiences are energetically stored in your body somewhere, somehow. Along with talk therapy, your child (and/or you) may benefit from some form of energy releasing technique to help the healing process. NET is quick and easy and helps release old stress and trauma with little effort. There has been quite a bit of research on the positive effects of NET on the symptoms of PTSD (post-traumatic stress disorder). Mackenzie and I have both been treated for PTSD, using this technique with great success.

A qualified NET practitioner uses a simple technique (similar to a minor chiropractic adjustment) to remove blocks in the body which can create a long list of physical and emotional problems, so the body can heal. Go to www.netmindbody.com to learn more. Call them if you can't find a practitioner listed in your area and they will assist you further.

Ho'oponopono (The Zero Point): Ho'oponopono, sometimes called *The Zero Point*, comes from an ancient Hawaiian prayer/statement that is used to manage and rectify errors in one's life. It's thought to be a mental cleansing that helps neutralize the energy around an issue that is imbalanced in one's life. Dr. Joe Vitalie wrote an interesting book about the technique called, *Zero Limit: The Secret Hawaiian System for Wealth, Health, Peace, and More (2007)*. I've used this technique for years when I'm feeling anxious and frustrated about something in my life and it really works for me. It's very simple. You just repeat the four statements; "I love you, I'm sorry, please forgive me, thank you" over and over in your head or out loud. Try it, and you may feel the calming effect it has on you and the situation.

Chiropractic Care: A chiropractor focuses on the diagnosis and treatment of the body as it relates to the neuromuscular system. A chiropractor's main focus is locating and releasing interferences in the nervous system that might be causing an illness or issue, and promoting the body's innate ability to heal itself. A typical chiropractor will "adjust" your spine and neurological system to help with whatever issue you present.

Chiropractic care is much more accepted by mainstream medicine, particularly with issues related to the body—not so much with issues related to emotions, though it may be paired with other techniques to address emotional issues such as anxiety and even mild depression. For this application, find a chiropractor who has further specialized training in techniques such as NET, Quantum Neurology, Applied Kinesiology, or Acupuncture, which address emotional issues. Dr. Jessica Riechert explains, "What I love about chiropractic medicine is that it helps the body move from a sympathetic state (excited, overwhelmed, highly charged) to a parasympathetic state (relaxed, grounded, calm). Most people walk around in a sympathetic state due to stress, environment toxics, food, or trauma. Chiropractic is an easy way to adjust your nervous system so it can slow down and heal."

Find an experienced chiropractor who graduated from an accredited program. Treatment can vary from gentle manipulation to more aggressive adjustment that feels almost like cracking the neck or the spine. Chiropractors with further training can also be a good source for nutritional counseling. Some insurance companies cover chiropractic care.

The Sedona Method: The Sedona Method is a simple, yet very effective tool for releasing unwanted feelings, ideas, and beliefs that are getting in the way of moving forward. It's a series of questions that lead you toward an energetic process that shifts your awareness about a current situation, thought, or emotion. The shift helps you accept and release your feelings and move forward. Melanie Smithson, an LPC and author of *Stress Free in 30 Seconds* (also a somatic psychotherapist and certified Sedona Method Coach) explains, "The Sedona Method allows the client to move through the negative self-beliefs and emotions that become embedded during a traumatic event(s) without re-telling the story and reliving the trauma. It's highly effective with children and adults. It's extremely efficient in the hands of a practiced clinician."

Look online to find a practitioner of the Sedona Method in your area. You can also learn it through books and/or recordings and practice it on yourself. Go to www.sedona.com for more information.

Acupuncture and Chinese Herbs: Acupuncture is based in the Chinese philosophy of energy flow in the body. It's a fascinating, complicated, and deep form of medicine. The mind-body connection is a very important part of the Chinese medicinal philosophy, and acupuncture can effectively help heal emotional imbalances such as anxiety, stress, insomnia, anger, grief, some depression, and even ADD. Be sure to find someone with experience in working with kids and teens and emotional issues.

Traditional Chinese medicine practitioners may also treat certain problems by using Chinese herbs, which can be very effective. Using herbs as part of a treatment protocol requires extensive training. More traditional practitioners will have you brew tea using a variety of herbs specific to the presenting problem, but some might give you capsules or pills. Acupuncturists can range from medical doctors trained in the U.S. or China to a certified and licensed practitioner from another field such as chiropractic or naturopathic medicine, who has taken a certain number of acupuncture classes. Check their training, credentials, and licensure. Some insurance companies now cover acupuncture.

Naturopathic Medicine: Naturopathic medicine is a broad form of medicine that uses natural forms of treatments first rather than prescription medications and surgeries. Most naturopaths are trained in nutrition and well-versed in vitamin supplements. Many will also use other forms of alternative treatments from light therapies, to ion cleanses, to energy balancing beds. I love the work of naturopaths because they look at the human body as a system of intricately related and interacting parts, and treat it as a whole. Often they suggest taking a lot of vitamins, which can get expensive. It might be very helpful to try out a naturopath for an opinion, particularly if you just can't find the source of your child's issues. Look for recommendations—some people swear by their naturopathic doctors; those are the ones you should see. Sadly, most insurance companies do not cover naturopathic medicine.

Reiki: There are many, many forms of energy healing; Reiki is one of the most common. During a Reiki treatment, the practitioner runs energy into the body of those they are treating (hands on or off the body), helping the body to restore its own physical and emotional well-being. Reiki is relaxing and can be very helpful. The skill and demeanor of the practitioner makes a huge difference in treatment. They should be well trained in all levels of Reiki and have experience with kids. A soft, gentle personality that shows compassion and kindness makes the Reiki experience that much better! To find a practitioner you can Google it in your area or go to www. reikimembership.com.

Pets: I love dogs and cats—most animals really. As a child, my dogs made me feel safe and secure in a complicated, unsafe world. Pets have many benefits to kids. They are trusted recipients of feelings/secrets, someone to talk to and feel safe with. Taking care of pets helps teach kids responsibility, nurturing, and even compassion. Family pets can create a common bond, a center for the family that everyone loves and enjoys. Pets will keep kids healthy by getting them moving and playing in nature. A friend whose teenage son struggles with socialization recently got his very own dog—he has full responsibility for the dog, which has given him a new sense of himself. He now has something to talk about, which allowed him to meet new people and step further out in the world on walks and hikes. It's been a real gift to a young man who needed the extra love, support, and self-awareness.

PART FIVE

Summary, More Imagine Stories, and References

In Closing

After my daughter, Mackenzie, was born extremely premature, I was overwhelmed, stressed, and traumatized. She was very sick for years with hospitalizations, surgeries, feeding tubes, oxygen, medications, monitors, OT, PT, ST, and the list goes on. It wasn't until many years later, when I received the proper help, that I realized I had Post-Traumatic Stress Disorder (PTSD) because of her early birth. My PTSD was compounded by my earlier trauma—my mom's suicide. I didn't understand what I was experiencing for years. My own traumas were causing me to be angry, anxious, feel shame, worry constantly, and feel unsure about myself in many areas of my life. Mackenzie and I had an abnormal bonding time early on, which complicated our relationship when she became a teenager. Thankfully, we found the proper help and both of us were able to heal and find a loving place to be together again. Healing is a process, it may take time, but it's always possible with the right help and understanding. Many of the tools in this book have come from my/our own trial and error, as well as a great deal of research in my personal and professional world.

Our kids are stressed. Many of them are traumatized too. All kids need a voice, and many need help. When we see a child hurting, we hurt. It's so hard to watch a child struggle, especially if we are attached to them emotionally. As I continue to travel and work with *The Imagine Project*™ in schools and organizations, I see how stressed and traumatized kids are in their young lives—far more than parents, teachers, and youth leaders may realize.

They need tools to help them deal with that stress. I hope a few things in this book will help you help them, particularly *My Imagine Journal™*. When life throws us challenges, all we can do is pull up our bootstraps, face those challenges, and move on.

As parents, we do our best to love our kids and give them everything we can to create a good quality life. Every family has a different idea of what that means. I hope this book helps you understand what your child is going through and offers tools to help your child rebalance and succeed in life, regardless of who they are and what they face. Always remember to ask yourself, "What part of my child's struggle might be mine?" Yes, the baggage we carry from our past will influence our parenting and family dynamic. If your child is struggling, think about the dynamic between the two of you. How do your own behaviors, ideas, and beliefs affect your relationship with your children? Your child, you, the two of you together, or even the entire family may need help getting through difficult times. Anything can be healed; I honestly believe that. I have seen it, felt it, known it. It takes time and work and sometimes outside help, but anything can be healed. It won't just go away on its own; you must be proactive in helping it heal. Using the tools and techniques in this book will help, and if you need more, seek outside help. It's courageous to step into your truth.

Teachers, you have a big job—a very difficult but extremely important job. We know that social-emotional wellness gives kids opportunities for learning and growth; in fact, learning and growth are almost impossible without emotional wellness. The suggestions in this book will give you some tools to help your students thrive, despite the challenges they may face in their lives.

When I was a nurse in the Neonatal Intensive Care, I loved to give parents one special piece of advice when they were taking their babies home from the hospital. "Be sure to take a moment every day to see your baby as absolutely perfect." I offered this guidance because amidst the chaos of dealing with "what's wrong" with someone, we often forget to see what's right. Please try it for yourself with your child, your student, or anyone in your care. Seeing them with your heart will reassure them too, that they are "just right," even when there are difficulties in life.

Take these suggestions and apply them in the ways that work best for your children, yourself, your spouse, students, clients, friends, and family. It's my dream that *The Imagine Project* will help heal the wounds of our children and in turn, make a positive impact on the world. Thank you for reading this book and caring about your own—and others'—emotional wellness.

More *Imagine* Stories from Kids

A 5ᵗʰ Grade Class, Ages 10-11

The stories from *The Imagine Project* are profound and give students, teachers, parents, and counselors a unique window into the minds and souls of individual children. It is difficult to get permission from parents so I opted to use a handful of stories from one 5ᵗʰ grade class (with permission). Keep in mind, these children are primarily from white, middle-class, well-educated families.

They may have a stronger foundation at home and at school than some children, but their stories demonstrate that they are not immune to enduring very stressful experiences, including divorce, serious illness and accidents, academic struggles, athletic disappointments, being bullied, and the death of a loved one or beloved pet. While these are real and difficult challenges, they are far less harrowing than the stories of at-risk kids, who are featured in the next section. Peter Hughes, a friend deeply involved in *The Imagine Project*, has commented that the stories from at-risk kids would "bring a giant to his knees."

Imagine...loving to go to school but struggling to read and learn.

Imagine...being afraid to raise your hand in class because you might be embarrassed and not know the answer.

Imagine...being taken to a doctor to see if there is something wrong with you.

Imagine...being diagnosed with something that means you have a hard time concentrating and thinking the same way other kids do.

Imagine...the doctor puts you on medication that helps you concentrate better.

Imagine...feeling like you can understand what you read better and you might just know the answer a teacher asks.

Imagine...feeling brave enough to raise your hand in class.

Imagine...being called on and KNOWING THE RIGHT ANSWER!

Imagine...seeing how happy your mom is when you go home and tell her how much better you are at reading.

Imagine...thinking you are as smart as the other kids and feeling proud of yourself!

Langston A.

~❧

Imagine...having a dog since the minute you were born.

Imagine...him being old, gentle, and caring but you hope he will live until your 10th birthday.

Imagine...getting an adorable puppy which bothers him but he decides to change.

Imagine...paying more attention to the puppy.

Imagine...not realizing that not paying as much attention to the older dog is one of the biggest mistakes you will ever make.

Imagine...the puppy is being taught by your older dog.

Imagine...putting down the older dog, knowing he was in pain.

Imagine...knowing you did the right thing and he is in a better place now but you still feel the pain inside you.

Imagine...your little puppy is growing very big now.

Imagine...knowing that you will never forget the older dog.

Imagine...walking away from that day feeling determined.

Imagine...being determined that you will treat your puppy just as nicely as the older dog.

Imagine...turning 11 in a month.

Imagine...feeling happy for your dog in heaven and knowing you two will meet again.

Imagine...knowing everything will be okay, and that's what your dog would want.

Imagine...realizing that you learned a lesson...always enjoy what you have, because before you know it, it will disappear because nothing is forever.

Keira M.

~✑

Imagine...your sister pushing you on your longboard and an ambulance racing down the hill about to hit you and stopping in front of your house.

Imagine...running in and seeing your dad on the ground struggling to get oxygen because he is really sick.

Imagine...going to your neighbor's house till your dad and mom get back from the E.R. and your sister throwing up because she is so scared.

Imagine...trying to fall asleep in your neighbor's house.

Imagine...finally getting a phone call from your mom at two in the morning telling you your dad is ok, he got a lot of fluids and he's ok.

Ryan C.

~✑

Imagine...loving school, your teacher, and all your friends.

Imagine...always getting A's and being one of the smartest kids in the class.

Imagine...not doing so well on a pop quiz.

Imagine...sitting at your desk staring at a test with no answers on it.

Imagine...being perplexed that you don't understand the math problems.

Imagine...feeling like you had a big cloud over your head that wouldn't go away.

Imagine...going home and you can't sleep, being stressed out of your mind, knowing you were going to get a bad score and it will affect your grade.

Imagine...going to school feeling sad and stressing so much.

Imagine...thinking how dumb you are and that you are never going to understand math.

Imagine...feeling embarrassed but still telling your teacher that you are baffled.

Imagine...your teacher explaining everything to you and now you understand all the questions.

Imagine...going to school happy again until one morning.

Imagine...going to school and seeing your friends give you dirty looks and make fun of you.

Imagine...hearing them say rude things about you behind your back but you heard them say every word.

Imagine...them knowing your bad scores on the test and tearing you down because you were confused.

Imagine...them bullying you every day for multiple reasons.

Imagine...every day being grim and all you are thinking about is the mean things they said about you.

Imagine...having sweaty palms and thoughts in your mind saying you can't do anything.

Imagine...coming to school sad now and not talking because if you did you felt like you would cry.

Imagine...knowing you are a great person but you are stuck in a deep dark hole and there is no way out.

Imagine...getting bad butterfly feelings in your stomach every day when you see your so-called friends.

Imagine...now locking up those feelings and being happy.

Imagine...having your family support you every day making you feel good about yourself.

Imagine...loving your blessing of a life and now that is history because you have loving people who helped you get through it.

Courtney G.

Imagine...a perfectly good day before Halloween.

Imagine...going out to dinner and leaving your cell phone at home so you wouldn't be distracted.

Imagine...getting home from dinner and rushing upstairs to grab your phone because you hear it going off.

Imagine...turning it on seeing 19 missed calls and texts coming from the same person.

Imagine...reading every text and looking out your window.

Imagine...seeing your best friend packing bags into her mother's car and driving away.

Imagine...breaking down, crying because you think you will never see them again.

Imagine...thinking this will ruin everything.

Imagine...two days later being able to FaceTime and call your friend again.

Imagine...finally seeing her in person for the first time in months.

Imagine...when you thought your life was ruined...it actually made everything better.

Kelsey F.

～❧

Imagine...having your parents on the phone all day every day and not knowing what is happening.

Imagine...you and your brother thinking something is up but still not knowing.

Imagine...hearing your parents fight every night and having an idea of what's happening.

Imagine...your parents telling you that you are all going to play whiffle ball.

Imagine...your parents telling you they aren't going to be married anymore.

Imagine...trying to play whiffle ball through all the sadness.

Imagine...going home and not knowing that your mom has been sleeping in the basement for months.

Imagine...crying every night because you think it's never going to get better.

Imagine...your mom telling you she got a new house.

Imagine...knowing that your dog won't be able to come to your new house.

Imagine...your mom moving out when your dad is on a business trip.

Imagine...trying to wake up every day saying, "It will be ok".

Imagine...your best friend moving 27 hours away from you.

Imagine...your brother telling you that it will be fine every day.

Imagine...getting up and knowing it will be okay.

Imagine...knowing that you have some great people who have your back even if they are 27 hours away.

Imagine...getting through everything with a happy attitude.

Ainslie M.

⁓ ∽⁊

Imagine...your rec coaches knowing you would be something special.

Imagine...the coaches having you try out for a team where the kids are older than you.

Imagine...thinking you could actually be something special.

Imagine...not knowing anyone at the tryouts and all you want is someone to comfort you.

Imagine...making a ton of mistakes and wishing you weren't there.

Imagine...waiting three days praying you will make the best team.

Imagine...hearing you made one of the worst teams.

Imagine...meeting the people who are on your team and knowing no one while they know each other.

Imagine...having all of them comfort you and knowing it will be alright.

Imagine...playing in tournaments all over Colorado.

Imagine...going to Disney World and Dallas, Texas for soccer.

Imagine...your team quitting and feeling colossally sad.

Imagine...starting all over.

Imagine...making an amazing friend and doing everything together except he made a better team than you.

Imagine...working blood, sweat, and tears trying to move up and play with him.

Imagine...playing your heart out and almost passing out.

Imagine...making the team with him*!*

Imagine...training your hardest each day and trying to make your dreams come true.

Imagine...being captain of your team and knowing you are one of the best!

Blake C.

Imagine...driving to the mountains for a family reunion.

Imagine...seeing beautiful trees and big buildings pass by while you watch a movie playing in the car.

Imagine...suddenly, seeing a car pull out in front of you and getting pulled forward in an instance.

Imagine...hitting the car in front of you and starting to cry as you hear the sounds of police sirens.

Imagine...seeing your dad speak with police, looking at people rush around, and speaking with firefighters who are wondering if you are ok or hurt.

Imagine...looking at your car, damaged, deplorable, and gruesome.

Imagine...your dad calling your aunt to come pick you up and take you to the reunion as he sorts it all out.

Imagine...getting in your aunt's car and watching your dad talk with the person driving the other car and the police as you slowly leave the scene.

Imagine...finally getting there and finding your dad not long behind you in the damaged car.

Imagine...your dad telling the story to you and your family, saying the person that hit you lied.

Imagine...having a great time at the reunion, and realizing that everything is ok!

Imagine...persevering and being determined through the whole process, even if you cried a little.

Imagine...forgetting all about the whole car crash and moving on with life.

Imagine...life not being perfect, but still finding hope in whatever it throws at you!

Ella P.

Imagine...waking up one day and getting told that your cousin might not live.

Imagine...not knowing why he was in intensive care.

Imagine...finding out that he was in the lane to turn left on his motorcycle and he got hit by a car and thrown 50 feet.

Imagine...getting a call saying that they were about to amputate his leg and that he would be in the hospital for a while.

Imagine...finally going to the hospital and hearing your great aunt yelling at the doctors and not knowing why.

Imagine...your great aunt finally calming down and telling us that the doctors overdosed our cousin and that his brain would never be the same again.

Imagine...your cousin being in a coma and not knowing if he would wake up again.

Imagine...your cousin finally waking up after three weeks and moving to a different hospital for rehab.

Imagine...your cousin getting a prosthetic leg and trying to learn how to put it on for the first time.

Imagine...your cousin learning how to talk and walk again.

Imagine...getting to go home for the first time in six months.

Imagine...his parents helping him find a home so he could live a normal life as an adult.

Imagine...living a full life after 17 years.

Imagine...living three minutes away from him and getting to visit him any time of the week.

Lauren T.

Alternative High School Teens

I was also able to get permission from a few teens at an Alternative High School Program. They too come from primarily white, educated, middle- to upper-class families, but as you'll see, they are not immune to trauma. Their stories offer insights into the plights of these kids, and can be difficult to read (they are unedited). Most of the positive *Imagines* are hopes they have for the future.

Read these with a compassionate heart and have faith in their journeys and their resilience.

Imagine...your parents divorcing at a young age.

Imagine...your mom taking your two dogs, sister, and "normal" life across the country.

Imagine...worrying about your amazing father's health.

Imagine...pleading for your mother to not take her life in front of you at an early age.

Imagine...three elementary, three middle, three high schools, and four homes, all decreasing in quality with each move.

Imagine...school with social anxiety and no friends.

Imagine...meeting the perfect girl day two of a new high school.

Imagine...changing who you are. Growing. Feeling happiness again. Getting good grades. Being an athlete again. Learning to love.

Imagine...an unforgettable end to a rough chapter.

Nick, grade 12

Imagine...finding out your dad going to jail the day before your 12th birthday for raping your two older sisters.

Imagine...being raped and finding out your best friend killed himself the day after.

Imagine...having to take what seems like millions of pills because you are told you aren't "sane" without them.

Imagine...having a miscarriage at 15.

Imagine...being diagnosed with so many mental illnesses that you can't even remember them all.

Imagine...dangling head first off of a building, regretting your decision, and not being able to pull yourself up.

Imagine...finding out that everything that you grew up with thinking was okay and "normal" is actually not.

Imagine...the last time you saw your dad, he molested you for the last time.

Imagine...having to go to the mental hospital 12 times for failed suicide attempts.

Imagine...living off of food stamps, and only being able to afford pancake mix and peanut butter for two years.

Imagine...being the first of your siblings to graduate.

Imagine...having a family of your own.

Imagine...being successful.

Imagine...having a good job.

Imagine...achieving all of your goals.

Imagine...being completely done with therapy in two months.

Felicia, grade 12

❧

Imagine...hearing from your family they want your grandpa dead.

Imagine...asking for help but no one listens.

Imagine...having your dad tell you to lie to the cops.

Imagine...your family telling you to kill yourself.

Imagine...your dad kicking you out right when you come home from school.

Imagine...making everything better again.
Imagine...showing everyone you changed.
Imagine...being a better person.

Elaine, grade 12

Imagine...living every day of your life afraid of
tomorrow.
Imagine...living every day depressed and suicidal.
Imagine...not knowing what you will do to yourself.
Imagine...living life not in control.
Imagine...feeling like you have nothing else to lose.
Imagine...losing all trust from your parents.
Imagine...your sister struggling as much as you do.
Imagine...using drugs to feel normal again.
Imagine...living every day of your life in pain.
Imagine...getting your dream car.
Imagine...being a mechanic.
Imagine...marrying a girl you love.
Imagine...getting over the pain.
Imagine...everything going right.

Justin, grade 12

Imagine...switching high schools four times.
Imagine...an abusive stepdad.
Imagine...your scars that have never really went away.
Imagine...you kept creating new scars to feel
something.

Imagine...feeling so alone you start doing drugs to make friends, drowning out how you really feel, and losing your true self.

Imagine...feeling so depressed you look to others for happiness, not finding your own.

Imagine...depending on them being happy so you could be too.

Imagine...your parents losing all trust in you and sending you to rehab.

Imagine...that everyone you thought were your "friends" just because you didn't want to get high.

Imagine...being left in the cold.

Imagine...finding yourself again through rehab, finding your support, finding that love you needed.

Imagine...finding teachers that cared and would listen to your story.

Imagine...making friends that really cared.

Imagine...knowing family loved you.

Imagine...finding your smile again.

Imagine...going to college.

Imagine...getting your associates degree in Drug and Counseling, maybe majoring in psychology.

Imagine...helping kids with drug addictions, just like you had.

Imagine...meeting the one person.

Imagine...living life knowing you did what you wanted.

Imagine...having no regrets.

Maci, grade 12

Imagine...seeing your dad abuse your mom.

Imagine...your dad slowly leave the picture as the divorce papers finalize.

Imagine...getting a new family and never expecting it.

Imagine...moving out of your childhood home while still a child.

Imagine...getting a new sister for the first time.

Imagine...your favorite sibling leave for the military.

Imagine...eating a late dinner by yourself and your sister attempts suicide upstairs.

Imagine...hearing her cry out while your family rushes to help.

Imagine...every morning you have to walk across her bloodstains that ate away at the carpet.

Imagine...opening the door at 2 am to a cop releasing information about your sister.

Imagine...cleaning out her room and finding drugs, knives, and cups of throw-up.

Imagine...not seeing your only (step)sister once in a blue moon until something bad comes up.

Imagine...texting a friend not knowing they were sent away.

Imagine...a year goes by and the only question they ask you is about your hair.

Imagine...crying over them.

Imagine...the time I tried to see a therapist she broke the code of not telling your parent.

Imagine...actual pain in your abdomen and doctors never figuring it out.

Imagine...your life goes to shit and gets better one year later.

Imagine...going to the Air Force to start your dream.

*Imagine...*later on going to countries, with high risk for war, to help the sick.

*Imagine...*helping enough people.

*Imagine...*having a different day, not behind a desk, but in a field.

*Imagine...*not helping famine and disease, but in one family's life you can change that, and still feeling great.

Lauren, grade 11

Teacher *Imagine* Stories

*Imagine...*having a career you deeply love, only to hear someone say, "Oh, you're just a teacher?"

*Imagine...*having 30 precious 5th graders depending on you to make their year count.

*Imagine...*every year, working more—for less.

*Imagine...*leaving school every day, but not the work—working an additional two to three hours each night preparing for the next day.

*Imagine...*greeting each student in the morning with a hug and love, because you truly care about each and every one of them.

*Imagine...*wanting more than anything to instill a love and passion for learning and confidence in every student.

*Imagine...*giving 110% of everything you have.

*Imagine...*researching creative ways to make learning meaningful and purposeful to a generation of students who get bored far more quickly than you've ever experienced.

Imagine...using the money you might have spent on a new pair of shoes to buy special treats or science equipment for the class.

Imagine...staying up past your bedtime to write a paper due for a class you must take to keep your license renewed.

Imagine...your highest performing student is three levels above grade level, and your lowest performing student is three levels below grade level, and there is a mixture in between, and you have to meet each individual need in reading, writing, math, science and social studies.

Imagine...trying to experiment with the latest trend in education, but still holding true to what you know really works.

Imagine...not sitting down all day because you are always "on", and being called in five different directions all day by kids who need your help.

Imagine...hearing from everyone, "You get the summers off—you should feel lucky!"

Imagine...spending your summers working a second job or taking more classes.

Imagine...feeling a student's hug and hearing she loves you.

Imagine...a student inviting you to watch her dance recital because she really wants you to be there.

Imagine...a student writing you a note telling you how much he loves learning from you.

Imagine...dancing and singing with your students while learning a new concept in science.

Imagine...wondering how to teach your struggling students to divide decimals and fractions, but noticing that after many tries and frustration, they get it.

Imagine...hearing from a parent that their student loves school now.

Imagine...hearing your former student became a teacher, because of you.

Imagine...being invited to college graduations from students you taught a decade ago.

Imagine...being proud of what your students have become.

Imagine...a student thanking you for believing in him.

Imagine...being a teacher, and not wanting to do anything else in the world.

Michelle Parker,
5th grade teacher

⁓☙

Imagine...being held back in second grade because your developmental indicators are not on par with that of your peers.

Imagine...being sent to another school the next year to repeat the second grade where you will be placed in a special pull out program where once a day you are in a class with other students who struggle academically.

Imagine...the confusion of being called "Flunker Frank" from classmates when they find out you had to repeat the same grade they are in.

Imagine...enduring a year of trauma from bullying, having only one friend (another one of the "special" kids) when the greatest excitement of your day was seeing your mother's car pulling up to take you home to a family that you knew loved you.

Imagine...the relief when realizing that next year when you get to start third grade back at your old school and realizing you will no longer have to face the kids who have determined you're not as smart as them. *Imagine*...making a pact with yourself that from now on, you will work extremely hard to blend in academically so your peers don't realize you're not as smart as them.

Imagine...continuing on into your secondary education doing everything you can to get C's in your classes, believing this will confirm to you and those around you that academically, at least you're average.

Imagine...figuring out how to work hard in and out of class to appear just as smart as your peers, and thinking the only ones who realized you weren't smart were your teachers who probably knew that what you lacked in intellect, you made up for in effort.

Imagine...starting to realize that rather than doing your school work just to get it done, but doing it to learn, made it much less intimidating and more interesting.

Imagine...realizing that the stuff that was stumping you, was also stumping the "smart kids", and suddenly you weren't just average, your report card was showing signs of above average, heck, on occasion you could even squeak out an A or two.

Imagine...having an English teacher in 11th grade who made you believe you were better than average and encouraged you to take the college writing course next year.

Imagine…five years later walking away from the University of Northern Colorado with a bachelor's degree in biology and the certification to teach secondary science in Colorado.

Imagine…the fear of now stepping away from the role of hard-working student, for whom things didn't come easily, to educational role model expected to inspire young people.

Imagine…having that first job at an inner city middle school where you would be responsible for the 6th grade science education of 140 students.

Imagine…having success that first year but still having insecurities which were ingrained into you, like being back in 2nd grade. Deciding to continue at least a few more years in education to see if this was your calling.

Imagine…a few more years turning into 28 years and still counting, teaching 6th grade science through 12th grade physics. Thousands of students have been through your classroom. Many have confidently navigated your coursework and pursued great things. However, it has always been that handful every year that enter your classroom with a fixed mindset that they are "not smart enough", or "need to blend in" that have kept you glued to this profession.

Imagine…how different your life would have been had you not gone through that second year of grade school labeled as a "flunkey". More importantly, imagine how much that handful of students you look forward to every year have benefited.

Mr. P.

Secondary Science teacher

Imagine...working hard to be the first in your family to attend college and deciding you wanted to make as much money as possible in international business.

Imagine...because of your faith in God, and solely because of that God and His love for you and his children, being told that you are going to be a teacher and work with teens, but not just any teens, the teens that are poverty stricken and that come from broken homes.

Imagine...barely making enough money to pay your bills, waking up at 4:30am five days a week to commute hours to communities where these teens are being marginalized more and more every year as gentrification takes over the homes their families have known for decades.

Imagine...having numerous teachers and staff you thought you could trust, who decide that they don't like you as a teacher and the hard work you were doing with students, and they attempt to make your work life even more difficult, attempt to get you fired...time and time again.

Imagine...your first year working with those teens and the dichotomy of the look in their eyes and the feelings they have for you: both hate and love; honor and disrespect.

Imagine...learning that not only do the majority of those teens read and write at least five years below grade level, but that they also could not care less about you and what you have to teach them, unless you work extremely hard to get to know them as people, as humans.

Imagine...being on a school bus coming back from a field trip and a female student starting to scream, then jumping over the bus seats, punching another female student in the face, and ripping out her weave.

Imagine...realizing these outbursts of violence, both physical and verbal, are common— in the classrooms, hallways, lunch room, and of course, right outside the school building.

Imagine...realizing that this behavior comes from the trauma they've experienced, a trauma that is repeated and perpetuated, again...and again...and again...from generation to generation, with no end in sight.

Imagine...seeing students beating each other up on a regular basis in the hallway and the bathrooms, initiating in you, the other teachers, the other staff and most sadly, the other students, that high anxiety, flight-or-fight response, taking hours at time for the feelings of anxiety to subside.

Imagine...knowing that the school-to-prison pipeline is a reality and not just a theory, especially in certain parts of the country.

Imagine...seeing the look on your students' faces when they say, after four of their five teachers have quit before Christmas, saying, "No one wants us Miss."

Imagine...two bright, beautiful, 13-year-old girls saying with sincerity in their voices, "We just want to learn and all we do every day is sit and play games on our iPads."

Imagine...realizing that you have the power to change this behavior and teach teens how to cope with that trauma, address that trauma, resolve that trauma and BREAK THE CYCLE of that trauma and of violence and hatred...all while helping them reach grade level in their reading and writing.

Imagine...having the power and experience to help students learn to not internalize the harm they cause to themselves and others when they act out in negative ways and teaching them healthy, positive, and constructive ways to express their feelings.

Imagine...working with other teachers that, similar to you, have the heart, stamina and resilience to "keep fighting the good fight."

Imagine...not quitting your career as a teacher despite insurmountable odds, challenges, despite more pay cuts, loss of health, despite extreme stress, long hours, even longer work weeks and slim chances of advancement.

Imagine...deciding to not quit your career as a teacher despite three-months of state standardized testing in addition to district standardized testing, despite principals who have never worked in a classroom and therefore cannot properly manage a school, despite feeling underappreciated and isolated...all because you know, as cliché as it sounds, YOU ARE MAKING A DIFFERENCE, ONE STUDENT AT A TIME.

Jordan Long, ELD
elementary, middle and high school

Imagine...entering the field as a young teacher with all the drive and energy in the world, knowing God gave you a heart for service.

Imagine...opening your first credit card account and accruing your first chunk of debt to prepare a learning space for the eager 7-year-old minds.

Imagine...spending nights and weekends working—consumed with planning, worry, ideas, and questions.

Imagine...criticism from peers.

Imagine...just graduating with a Bachelor's Degree and continuing to take classes so you can be the one to make a difference for kids.

Imagine...researching poverty, gifted students, Autism, emotions, dyslexia, learning styles, classroom strategies and more to try to meet ALL kids where they are.

Imagine...having a fiancé your first year teaching who calls you at 6 PM to remind you to go home and eat.

Imagine...vacillating back and forth between feeling worn out by the daily events you face and trying to make a difference.

Imagine...knowing the little things make a difference.

Imagine...reflecting after ten years and realizing what an impossible job you've taken on for a decade now.

Imagine...feeling so burnt out you desire a change.

Imagine...continuing to volunteer for committees, take classes, earn your Masters, plan meticulously, carefully implement the most effective strategies you've learned, try to meet the basic and emotional needs of some students while also trying to extend learning opportunities for others.

Imagine...never letting up because you know it makes a difference or plants a seed for a young mind, maybe two.

Imagine...being pregnant with your first baby, only to find out you're having two babies amid your commitment to teaching. Now where does my time go? You have to work to make ends meet.

Imagine...juggling it all.

Imagine...realizing you've earned a Master's Degree but live paycheck to paycheck.

Imagine...remembering we have so much more than so many others in the world.

Imagine...waking up every day loving your family, finding the gratitude each day, and working hard to make a difference in a young heart and head.

Imagine...never knowing if you've made a difference.

Imagine...realizing you have!

Sam Alexander,
3rd grade teacher

~✜

Imagine...entering the world of teaching with child-like faith and arms open wide to possibilities.

Imagine...believing that you have what it takes to make a difference in children's lives and showing up every day with enthusiasm and optimism.

Imagine...quickly discovering that teaching is more complicated than you thought.

Imagine...realizing that before you can teach math or reading or writing, you have to teach love.

Imagine...seeing a classroom full of little people who are starving for attention.

Imagine...finding a need to reach down deep inside each individual student to hear their stories.

Imagine...guiding students through the process of acknowledging their own struggles, gratitude, and dreams.

Imagine...watching as children find power within themselves to overcome, to thrive, and to make a difference.

Imagine...observing the transformation from despair to hope as Imagine stories heal each individual writer and inspire understanding, kindness, and compassion in others.

Imagine...believing, once again, that what you do every day IS making a difference.

Lauren (Lionetti) Zuiker,
2nd grade teacher

Lauren (Lionetti) Zuiker,
2nd grade teacher

~❧

Imagine...growing up knowing that your role in this world is to contribute to the next generation.

Imagine...landing your dream job as a science teacher, but moving 2000 miles away from everything you know and love.

Imagine...being 26 years old and trusted to coach a sport you have never coached before.

Imagine...going home most days feeling you have failed your athletes, but vowing to work harder and be better tomorrow.

Imagine...turning this part-time gig into the center of your life.

Imagine...discovering your athletes not only have talent, but they also have integrity, commitment, and they believe in your coaching.

Imagine...watching the kids do everything you ask of them and still not be able to fulfill the potential you saw in them.

Imagine...lying in bed at night, with your intrinsic pressure to succeed keeping you awake.

Imagine...sitting in a gymnastics training center with a few athletes on a cold winter night, learning a relaxation process called EFT (tapping).

Imagine...discreetly pulling aside a few of your most trusted runners to teach them this new technique.

Imagine...catching a glimpse of your senior captain using EFT at the start line of the biggest race of the season.

Imagine...watching him race with every fiber of his being to a comeback victory that changes the culture of your program.

Imagine...losing your mind when your top female runner skips her usual physiological warm-up to tap herself to race readiness.

Imagine...cheering with amazement as she runs the bravest 800 meters you have ever witnessed, fighting through physical trauma and mental barriers by racing with her heart more than her legs.

Imagine…using tapping as a way to keep another runner running instead of killing himself, by convincing him his life is worth living.

Imagine…seeing your student leaders teaching your rookies about tapping, without any provocation from you.

Imagine…having enough confidence in your coaching to let that happen.

Imagine…teaching tapping to 150+ squirrelly middle-school athletes in a crowded basketball gymnasium.

Imagine…listening to them react with shouts of amazement when they discover how truly powerful it is.

Imagine…sweating through your button-up shirt before presenting your "coaching philosophy" to the top coaches in the state.

Imagine…tapping your head furiously underneath the stairs in the hallway.

Imagine…finishing your talk with a group tapping session, brave enough to share your fears with your community.

Imagine…knowing you have cultivated a powerful process to find clarity and focus in your own life and the lives of hundreds of excited and capable students and athletes.

Brian Seppala,
8th grade Science Teacher and Track Coach.
(see more about EFT/tapping in chapter 11)

Imagine…knowing in eighth grade that you wanted to be a social worker and never wavering, not once.

Imagine...realizing that there will never be an end to the need.

Imagine...being there with a client when she finds out she is pregnant, sharing the excitement of the full term pregnancy, and being by her side when she buries her infant son after he had been violently shaken by her boyfriend.

Imagine...realizing that you can't help everyone when you call a client's psychiatrist to check in on your client, just to find out that the psychiatrist is about to give the eulogy at your client's funeral after his suicide.

Imagine...wondering if there was something you could have done.

Imagine...talking students through their traumatic memories and feeling you were right there with them when it happened.

Imagine...having a student trust you with painful secrets.

Imagine...having a student use your phone because they want to call their mom who hasn't been home for five days and they're worried.

Imagine...having your student fall asleep during class, close to the nearest heat register, because they haven't slept well in days because there is no heat at home.

Imagine...calling a student's home to speak with a parent about the child's drug use only to find out that the parents are supplying the drugs and allowing the student to use them.

Imagine…a half burnt candle as a Christmas gift, one
of the best presents you have ever received, from
a student just wanting to say you are important to
him.

Imagine…teaching 25 students who haven't had much
luck in school before but are willing to give it another try in an alternative high school.

Imagine…seeing them "melt" as they realize that school
may be a good place after all.

Imagine…being under the impression that you are a
teacher but quickly realizing you are a student.

Imagine…having the opportunity to make a difference.

Imagine…talking them through everyday so that
the end is always in sight and graduation is a
possibility.

Imagine…marking off another day towards that goal
with the big red "X," day after day.

Imagine…the joy in their faces when that day finally
comes, the absolute thrill of accomplishment and the
sense of validation.

Imagine…students calling you out by name in an au-
ditorium of 200 people because they want to thank
you for "never giving up on them" and "always being
there for them."

Imagine…crying tears of happiness and tears of sadness all at once: happy to see them finish, sad to see
them fly away.

Imagine…fearing that you haven't reached them…then
realizing that you made a difference.

Diane Fern, MSW,
Alternative Program Teacher

Imagine...knowing from a very young age that children made your heart full.

Imagine...having the career of your dreams...teaching children.

Imagine...after 25 years of teaching you still love going to work every day.

Imagine...getting constant hugs from precious 5 year olds.

Imagine...watching children light up when they figure out they are reading, writing, or doing math and they say... "I did it!" Or "I can do it!" with a smile that lights up the room.

Imagine...making a difference in hundreds of children's lives by loving them, teaching them, and giving them the confidence that they can accomplish anything.

Imagine...having students come back when they are in middle school or high school to shadow you so they can go into the teaching field.

Imagine...giving and receiving unconditional love every day!

Imagine...being invited to birthday parties, first communions, bar mitzvah's, high school graduations, and weddings of students you had in kindergarten.

Imagine...the gratefulness, joy, and love I experience every day because of 5 year olds.

Imagine...touching the hearts and minds of our future...a president, someone finding a cure for cancer, a teacher, because they want to make a difference.

Imagine...being a teacher!

Amy Ford,
Kindergarten teacher

Parent *Imagine* Stories

Imagine...having gone through early menopause, taking birth control to regulate your hormones, and finding yourself pregnant at the age of 39.

Imagine...realizing what a blessing this new child will be and how much his spirit must have wanted to be in my family to conceive under such odds. God has truly sent me a blessing.

Imagine...having a husband being thrown into extreme bipolar and psychotic episodes because my pregnancy brought up his own childhood trauma.

Imagine...divorcing my husband when my sweet child was 5 years of age because conditions at home became life threatening for me and my two older children.

Imagine...the fear of leaving this marriage with no money and no income to support me and my 3 children.

Imagine...doing everything possible to maintain a sense of "normalcy" for my children while starting a business, racking up basic living expenses on credit cards, and being harassed and threatened by my ex-husband.

Imagine...watching this small child trying to understand what is happening in his family, not knowing what to believe and feeling there is no outlet for his feelings so he just bottles them up inside.

Imagine...bringing home a little puppy to give this child... a friend to talk to talk to and play with... because there seems to be no other way to reach this beautiful child.

Imagine...the helpless feeling as you watch this child try to hide from the world and escape. He begins to explore the world of drugs and alcohol...you fear he may get lost in this underworld and not find his way home. You fear the loss of this child and have the determination to do everything possible to save him from himself.

Imagine...this child gets caught by police on a minor charge and the judge sees the big picture and gives him a harsh sentence in an attempt to deter him.

Imagine...your life in chaos, attempting to keep a business on track, start a new business, help this child through his court dates, court requirements and drug tests, show him how much he is loved and supported...while this child scoffs at you and all authority.

Imagine...feeling the cancer begin to grow in your body, again, because of the stress in your life, and trying to find ways to take care of yourself and support your son.

Imagine...the painful realization that this beautiful child has chosen a more challenging path than you would have wished for him. He has dropped out of high school and is failing his court-ordered drug tests.

Imagine...knowing if he doesn't turn around his life the judge will send him to jail and his life will forever be changed in ways he can't even imagine.

Imagine...this teen finally realizes he is on a path that is destroying his life today, and his future.

Imagine…peacefully coexisting with a son who realizes that his actions are harming more than himself.

Imagine…he finally accepts your love and encouragement, and is respecting you and your rules.

Imagine…he begins to study and passes all his GED courses.

Imagine…the relief and pride as you see him get and keep a job, continue his education in college and begin to dream of a future that will support him and fill him with love, joy and a sense of self worth.

Imagine…the joy in your heart when he is grown and realizes how much he is loved and how he knows his mother always has and always will support him in every way possible.

Imagine…knowing that my son is a great and beautiful blessing from God.

Patty, mom to John

~❧

Imagine…being 21 years old in an abusive relationship, leaving your husband of 4 months and thinking "Thank God I got out before something really bad happened."

Imagine…several weeks later finding out you are pregnant. The judge won't grant the divorce until after the baby comes. He thinks the baby may change the situation and the marriage might work… it doesn't.

Imagine…being the single mother of a 6-month old son who was thriving and now he is struggling to eat, sit up, roll over or crawl.

*Imagine...*sitting in Sunday mass, your child sleeping peacefully in your arms and as he wakes up he starts jerking violently.

*Imagine...*hearing the Neurologist say, "Your son has a rare seizure disorder; there have only been 18 diagnosed cases to date."

*Imagine...*being told that your son will most likely die before he is 3 years old.

*Imagine...*your parents, siblings and entire extended family reeling from this news; having no idea what we are dealing with.

*Imagine...*learning how to give your child injections to control his seizures, and instead of helping, it causes him to swell up beyond recognition, and the seizures won't stop.

*Imagine...*choosing to try an "experimental diet" to save your son's life, having surgery to insert a feeding tube; knowing your son will most likely be fed through that tube for the rest of his life.

*Imagine...*none of the drugs, therapies, diet ingredients, or critical supplies being covered by insurance because they are considered "experimental."

*Imagine...*struggling to pay bills, and worrying about how to keep a roof over your head because your money has to pay for all of your son's critical medical needs.

*Imagine...*the most amazing resource center in your state providing in-home therapies, listening to your fears, giving encouragement, and connecting you with resources that will start covering the costs of your son's critical needs.

Imagine...your son becoming stable enough to take a bus to a special school and start engaging with other children.

Imagine...your son being included in everything, not just the multitude of therapies, but community involvement, trips to the zoo, picnics in the park, swimming, dances, celebrations, and holiday programs.

Imagine...family, friends, and those at the resource center accepting your son as "perfect just the way he is".

Imagine...yourself accepting your son as "perfect just the way he is".

Imagine...meeting the love of your life and knowing he loves your son as much as he loves you..

Imagine...blending your families and watching how happy your son is. He has a smile that can light up the world!

Imagine...Cameron, now 34 years old.

Imagine...knowing that even though your son is profoundly impacted—he will never talk, eat, walk, or be able to take care of himself—he is the <u>embodiment of LOVE</u>.

Imagine...he will never judge, he will never complain, he will never whine, he will NEVER HATE!

Imagine...being the parent of a child who every waking hour of every day only knows how to LOVE.

Susan, mom to Cameron

Imagine...being pregnant with your 3ʳᵈ child, the long-awaited little girl.

Imagine...the joy.

Imagine...discovering at 22 weeks that your amniotic fluid level is low—the doctor being unconcerned and saying to go rest and drink lots of water.

Imagine...taking a short trip into the mountains, where you can rest.

Imagine...noticing blood and rushing to the hospital in a small mountain town.

Imagine...the doctor telling you there is nothing they can do; the baby isn't developed enough—just go home and let nature run its course.

Imagine...your husband driving like a madman in the middle of the night to get you back to the big city and a hospital that can take care of your baby if she is born.

Imagine...being confined to strict bed rest in the hospital, leaving 2 little boys at home.

Imagine...ten days later, celebrating your 35ᵗʰ birthday in the hospital, visited by your 2 little boys and husband, and your water breaking and the contractions worsening.

Imagine...two hours later, you and your baby suddenly sharing the same birthday.

Imagine...this birth happening way too soon, your tiny baby being born weighing only 1 pound, 12 ounces.

Imagine...the fear.

Imagine...being told, "We really don't know how she

will do; if she survives, she has a very high risk of many long-term problems."

Imagine...naming her, not knowing whether she'll live or die. Mackenzie Irene.

Imagine...having been a neonatal intensive care nurse yourself, for 11 years, and now experiencing the other side, *as a parent.*

Imagine...watching over *everything* the doctors and nurses do—focusing on what's wrong instead of what's right.

Imagine...the worry.

Imagine...months of ups and downs, near-death illnesses, IV's, X-rays, tube feedings, not being able to hold and bond with your little girl.

Imagine...your baby not taking a bottle because she is afraid of food in her mouth.

Imagine...being told by professionals not to hold her or look at your baby while feeding her because it's too overwhelming for her.

Imagine...finally bringing her home, hoping the ups and downs will taper off, but instead they worsen.

Imagine...still not being able to hold your baby, look at her, and smile as you feed her. Being told to put her on the couch facing away from you to give her a bottle.

Imagine...more hospitalizations, serious illnesses, surgeries, oxygen for 3 ½ years, feeding tubes for 5 years, plus physical therapy, occupational therapy, speech therapy, and intravenous therapy for years.

Imagine...being unable to cope, post-traumatic stress disorder (PTSD) hitting hard.

Imagine...the anger, sadness, fear, confusion, and feeling overwhelmed.

Imagine...family stepping in and helping.

Imagine...your baby growing, smiling, and beating the odds.

Imagine...your baby becoming the most beautiful girl, with a smile that lights up the room.

Imagine...watching her struggles in school and socially—not knowing how to help.

Imagine...trying every tool, method, and idea you can think of to help her (and yourself).

Imagine...her teenage years being the hardest because she is confused about herself, her life, and her relationship with you.

Imagine...she moves away to Nashville to go to art school, having a natural eye for beauty.

Imagine...she slowly begins to find herself.

Imagine...the ups and downs of your relationship with each other—complicated by the strains of her early life.

Imagine...the guilt.

Imagine...spending your birthdays together every year, and realizing you are both still so wounded.

Imagine...finally realizing you are both dealing with PTSD from her premature birth.

Imagine...getting help.

Imagine...healing.

Imagine...watching your little girl develop into a healthy, caring, confident, wise, creative, and talented young woman.

Imagine...seeing, feeling, knowing your relationship is

growing in love, light, and a deeper understanding of each other.

Imagine...the pride, peace, and love you feel as you watch her—wishing you could go back in time and tell yourself not to worry, it's all going to be okay.

Imagine...sharing your wisdom with others so they can learn from your experiences.

Imagine...the gifts of life.

Imagine...the gratitude.

Dianne, mom to Mackenzie Irene

REFERENCES AND RESOURCES

Chapter 1: Emotional Wellness

Durlak J, Weissberg R, Dymnicki A, Taylor R, Schellinger K. The Impact of Enhancing Students' Social and Emotional Learning: A Meta-Analysis of School-Based Universal Interventions. *Child Development* [serial online]. January 2011;82(1):405-432. Available from: Psychology and Behavioral Sciences Collection, Ipswich, MA. Accessed June 27, 2017.

Hoffman, D. M. (2009). Reflecting on social emotional learning: A critical perspective on trends in the United States. *Review of Educational Research June 2009, Vol. 79, No. 2, pp. 533–556 DOI: 10.3102/0034654308325184. 2009 AERA. http://rer.aera.net.*

Pert, C. (1997). *Molecules of Emotion; The Science Behind Mind-Body Medicine.* New York: Scribner.

Seigel, D.J. (2016). *No Drama Discipline: The Whole-Brain Way to Calm the Chaos and Nurture Your Child's Developing Mind.* New York: Bantam Books.

Seigel, D.J. (1999). *The Developing Mind: How Relationships and The Brain Interact to Shape Who We Are.* New York: Guilford Press.

Weissberg, R. (2016, February 15). Why Social and Emotional Learning Is Essential for Students. Retrieved July 28, 2017, from https://www.edutopia.org/blog/why-sel-essential-for-students-weissberg-durlak-domitrovich-gullotta

Chapter 2: Stress

Allan, J. (2007). *Creating Welcoming Schools: A Practical Guide to Home-school Partnerships.* Newark, DE: International Reading Association.

APA annual stress survey finds teens more stressed than adults. (2014). *Brown University Child & Adolescent Behavior Letter, 30*(5), 4-5.

Bethune, Sophie, (2014), *American Psychological Association Survey Shows Teen Stress Rivals That of Adults.* Accessed March, 2017. http://www.apa.org/news/press/releases/2014/02/teen-stress.aspx

Edutopia: www.edutopia.org. Sharing evidence and practitioner-based learning strategies to improve K-12 education in all areas, including social-emotional learning, project based, and creating a community of learners. Accessed July 1, 2017.

Shapiro, L.E. & Sprague, R.K. (2009). *The Relaxation and Stress Reduction Workbook for Kids: Help for Children to Cope with Stress, Anxiety, and Transitions (Instant Help)* Canada: Rain Coast Books.

Smithson, M. (2014). *Stress Free in 30 Seconds.* Denver: Komodia Press.

www.teachthought.com is a resource for teachers with activity ideas for getting to know your students, best books to teach empathy and other great information.

Chapter 3: Trauma

Garrett, K. (2014). Childhood Trauma and Its Affects on Health and Learning. *Education Digest, 79*(6), 4.

Levine, P. & Kline, M. (2007). *Trauma Through A Child's Eyes: Awakening the Ordinary Miracle of Healing.* Berkeley, CA: North Atlantic Books.

Meiners, C.J. (2010). *Cool Down and Work Through Anger.* Minnesota: Free Spirit Publishing.

Rothschild, B. (2000). *The Body Remembers: The Psychology of Trauma and Trauma Treatment.* New York, W. W. Norton & Co.

Shalka, T. R. (2015). Toward a Trauma-Informed Practice: What Educators Need to Know. *About Campus, 20*(5), 21-27. doi:10.1002/abc.21217

Souers, K., & Hall, P. A. (2016). *Fostering resilient learners: Strategies for creating a trauma-sensitive classroom.* Alexandria, VA: ASCD.

Sporleder, J. & Forbes, H.T. (2016). *The Trauma-Informed School: A Step-by-Step Implementation Guide for Administrators and School Personnel.* Boulder, Colorado: Beyond Consequences Institute, LLC.

Stahl, B. & Goldstein, E. (2010). *A Mindfulness-Based Stress Reduction Workbook.* New Harbinger).

Terrasi, S., & de Galarce, P. C. (2017). Trauma and learning in America's classrooms. *Phi Delta Kappan, 98*(6), 35. doi:10.1177/0031721717696476

Truman, K.K. (1991). *Feelings Buried Alive Never Die.* St. George, Utah: Olympus Distributing.

Van Der Kolk, B. (2014). *The Body Keeps Score.* New York: Penguin Books.

Verdick, E. & Lisovskis, M. (2015). *How to Take the Grrrr Out of Anger.* Minnesota: Free Spirit Publishing.

Chapters 4 and 5: Expressive Writing and *The Imagine Project Journal*

Baikie, K. & Wilhelm, K. (2005). Emotional and physical health benefits of expressive writing. *Advances in Psychiatric Treatment*, (11), 338-346.

Brown, B. (2013). *Daring greatly: How the Courage to be Vulnerable Transforms the Way We Live, Love, Parent, and Lead.* London: Penquin Books, Ltd..

Brown, B. (2017). *Rising Strong.* New York: Random House.

Gruwell, E. (2009). *The Freedom Writers Diary: How a Teacher and 150 Teens Used Writing to Change Themselves and The World Around Them.* New York: Broadway Books.

Gruwell, E. (2007). *The Freedom Writers Diary Teachers Guide.* New York: Broadway Books.

No Nonsense Nurturing: http://www.ct3education.com/no-nonsense-nurturer

Pennebaker, J.W. & Evans, J.F. (2014) *Expressive Writing: Words that Heal.* (Washington: Idyll Arbor).

Pennebaker, J.W. & Smyth, J.M. (2016). *Opening Up by Writing It Down, Third Edition: How Expressive Writing Improves Health and Eases Emotional Pain.* (New York: Guilford Press).

Restorative Justice in the Classroom: https://www.edutopia.org/blog/restorative-justice-resources-matt-davis

Weinman, J., Ebrecht, M., Scott, S., Walburn, J., & Dyson, M. (2008). Enhanced wound healing after emotional disclosure intervention. *British Journal of Health Psychology*, *13*(1), 95-102.

Chapter 6: The Mind

Buron, K.D. (2013). *When My Worries Get Too Big!:* Kansas: AAPC Publishing.

Braden, G. (2014). *Resilience from the Heart: The Power to Thrive in Life's Extreme.:* Carlsbad, CA: Hayhouse.

Choquette, S. (1999). *The Wise Child: A Spiritual Guide to Nurturing Your Child's Intuition.* New York: Three Rivers Press.

Currie, L. (2014). 8 Reasons Why Kindness Should Be Taught in Schools. *Psych Central.* Retrieved on May 1, 2017, https://psychcentral.com/blog/archives/2014/05/02/8-reasons-why-kindness-should-be-taught-in-schools/

Cuyler, M., & Yoshikawa, S. (2007). *Kindness is cooler, Mrs. Ruler.* New York: Simon & Schuster Books for Young Readers.

Crist, J.J. (2004). *What to Do When You're Scared and Worried: A Guide for Kids.* Minnesota: Free Spirit Publishing.

Dispenza, J., & Amen, D. G. (2015). *Breaking the habit of being yourself: how to lose your mind and create a new one.* Carlsbad, CA: Hay House.

The Greater Good Project at UC Berkeley provides science-based practices for a meaningful life, including mindfulness, resilience to stress, compassion, and kindness. www.greatergood.berkeley.edu

Greenland, S.K. (2010). *The Mindful Child: How to Help Your Kid Manage Stress and Become Happier, Kinder, and More Compassionate.* New York: Free Press.

Forsyth, J.P. & Eifert, G.H. (2007). *The Mindfulness and Acceptance Workbook for Anxiety: A Guide to Breaking Free from Anxiety, Phobias, and Worry Using Acceptance and Commitment.* New Harbinger Publications, Inc.

Hamilton, D. (2000). *Why Kindness is Good for You.* United Kingdom: Hay House.

Hay, L.L. (1984). *You Can Heal Your Life.* United States: Hay House.

The HeartMath Institute provides tools to help individuals connect to their own and others' hearts for stress reduction, social fulfillment and to facilitate a shift in global consciousness. www.heartmath.org

Lambrecht R.W. (2017) *Parenting at Your Best: Powerful Reflections and Straightforward Tips for Becoming a Mindful Parent* Castle Rock: Three Hearts Press.

Lipton, B. (2005). *Biology of Belief.* Santa Rosa, CA: Mountain of Love/Elite Books.

Craver, M. M., & Pinelli, A. (2012). *Chillax!: how Ernie learns to chill out, relax, and take charge of his anger.* Washington, DC: Magination Press.

Sounds True website: http://www.soundstrue.com/store/

Teasdale, J.D., William DPhil, J.M., Segal, Z.V., (2014). *The Mindful Way Workbook: An 8-Week Program to Free Yourself from Depression and Emotional Distress.* New York: Guildford Press.

Chapter 7: The Body

Boyd, D. (2015). *It's Complicated: The Social Lives of Networked Teens.* United States: Yale University Press.

Breathe for Change is a yoga training program exclusively for educators www.breatheforchange.com

Brown, S. & Vaughan, C. (2010). *Play: How it Shapes the Brain, Opens the Imagination, and Invigorates the Soul.* New York: Avery.

Cohen, D. *Why Kids to Spend more Time in Nature.* https://childmind.org/article/why-kids-need-to-spend-time-in-nature/. Accessed March, 2017.

Fallon, S. (2001). Nourishing Traditions: The Cookbook that Challenges Politically Correct Nutrition and Diet Dictocrats. Newtrends Publishing, Inc.

Fuhrman, J. (2011). *Eat to Live*. Boston: Little, Brown and Co.

Gaia TV has a channel devoted to yoga, in addition to other personal development channels www.gaiatv.com

Greenland, S.K. (2016). *Mindful Games: Sharing Mindfulness and Meditation with Children, Teens, and Families*. New York: Free Press.

Goldman, D., Bennett, L. and Barlow, Z. (2012). *Ecoliterate: How educators are cultivating emotional, social and ecological intelligence*. San Francisco: Jossey-Bass.

Kok Sui, M. C. (2005). *Superbrain Yoga*. Phillipines: Institute for Inner Studies Publishing Foundation, Inc.

Louv, R. (2008). *Last Child in the Woods: Saving our Children from Nature-Deficit Disorder*. Chapel Hill, NC: Algonquin Books.

Perlmutter, D. (2015). *Grain Brain: The Surprising Truth About Wheat, Carbs, and Sugar—Your Brains Silent Killers*. Place of publication not identified: Little Brown.

Shetreat-Klein, M., & Holtzman, R. (2016). *The Dirt Cure: Growing Healthy Kids with Food Straight From the Soil*. New York: Atria Books.

Chapter 8: The Spirit

Cameron, J. (2016). *The Artist's Way: A Spiritual Path to Higher Creativity*. London: Macmillan.

Gilbert, P. (2011). *Spirituality and Mental Health: A Handbook for Service Users, Careers and Staff Wishing to Bring a Spiritual Dimension to Mental Health Services*. Brighton: Pavillion Publishing, Ltd..

Kirp, D. L. (2014, January 12). Meditation transforms roughest San Francisco schools. Retrieved July 28, 2017, from http://www.sfgate.com/opinion/openforum/article/Meditation-transforms-roughest-San-Francisco-5136942.php

Nye, R. (2009). *Children's Spirituality: What it is and Why it Matters (Sure Foundations).* London: Church House Publishing.

Ramsburg, J. T., & Youmans, R. J. (2013). Meditation in the Higher-Education Classroom: Meditation Training Improves Student Knowledge Retention during Lectures. *Mindfulness, 5*(4), 431-441. doi:10.1007/s12671-013-0199-5

Starting A Classroom Meditation Practice. (2015, May 18). Retrieved July 27, 2017, from http://choices.scholastic.com/blog/starting-classroom-meditation-practice.

Tolson, C.L. & Koenig, H.G. (2003). *The Healing Power of Prayer.* Grand Rapids, MI: Baker Books.

Wallace, C. (November 10, 2015). How to Help Your Kids Find a Purpose. (n.d.). Retrieved April 21, 2017, from http://time.com/4105664/how-to-help-your-kids-find-a-purpose/ http://time.com/4105664/how-to-help-your-kids-find-a-purpose/.

Williamson, M. (2016). *Tears to Triumph: The Spiritual Journey from Suffering to Enlightenment.* (New York: HarperOne).

Chapters 9 and 10, Extra Help and Therapies
Parents

These two indispensible resources offer key information about viewing child behavior and emotions in the context of the child's developing brain, plus how to guide your children and teens in ways that promote good brain development *and* a loving relationship with you, which is the key to your child adopting good behavior, being well-adjusted, and creating a happy, healthy life.

Bradley, M. *Yes Your Teen is Crazy: Loving Your Kid Without Losing Your Mind.* Harbor Press, 2002.

Siegel, D. J. and Bryson, T.P. *No-Drama Discipline: The Whole-Brain Way to Calm the Chaos and Nurture Your Child's Developing Brain.* Bantam Books, 2014.

Download, print, and post these handy reminders on how to connect and redirect: http://www.drdansiegel.com/pdf/ Refrigerator%20Sheet--NDD.pdf

Teachers

These resources offer important practical guidance as well as inspiration for the incredible job you do.

Nelson, J. *Positive Discipline: The Classic Guide to Helping Children Develop Self-Discipline, Responsibility, Cooperation, and Problem-Solving Skills.* Balantine Books, 2006. https://www.positivediscipline.com/

Nieto, S. (2003). *What keeps teachers going?* New York: Teachers College Press.

The documentary film *TEACH* (2013), by director Davis Guggenheim, explores what it takes to be a teacher, following actual teachers as they continue a process of ongoing professional learning and teaching. Website: http://www.takepart.com/teach/film/index.html View it here: https://www.youtube.com/watch?v=y_TKuwm2ysA

Holistic Wellness

The following physicians have had a significant impact on how medicine is perceived and practiced in an integrative, holistic approach. Each is an M.D. and an author, and each has a great deal to offer in terms of wellness. See their websites and for more information: Dr. Christiane Northrup, www.drnorthrup.com; Dr. Lissa Rankin, www.lissarankin. com; and Dr. Andrew Weil, www.drweil.com.

Chapter 11: Complementary Therapies

Biodynamic CranioSacral Therapy: https://www. craniosacraltherapy.org

EFT Tapping and Training: The Art, Science and Business of Tapping. http://www.efttappingtraining.com/category/articles/

Homeopath Sue Boorn (also does long-distance consultations): http://homeopathydenver.com

Homeopath Steve Waldstein (also does long-distance consultations): http://homeopathy-cures.com

Jain, R. (2015). *Tapping for Zapping Anxiety Away: Go Tapping! Nelly Learns the Emotional Freedom Technique (EFT) for Kids*. GoStrengths, Ltd.

Lite, L. (2011). *Angry Octopus: An Anger Management Story Introducing Active Progressive Muscular Relaxation and Deep Breathing*. Stress Free Kids.

NET: A Mind Body Stress Reduction Technique: https://www.netmindbody.com

Ortner, N. (2013). *The Tapping Solution: A Revolutionary System for Stress-Free Living*. United States: Hay House.

Quantum Neurology: http://quantumneurology.com

Rhymes, D. (2016). *Kids EFT Tapping: A Self-Help Tool for Life*. Olite Publishing.

Vitalie, J. (2007). *Zero Limit: The Secret Hawaiian System for Wealth, Health, Peace, and More*. Hoboken, New Jersey: John Wiley & Sons.

DIANNE MARONEY IS A Clinical Nurse Specialist in Psychiatric/Mental Health Nursing. She is a thought leader in the area of stress and trauma in children, and founded *The Imagine Project, Inc.*, a nonprofit organization that helps kids, teens, and adults overcome challenging life circumstances through expressive writing. Dianne developed a simple yet profound 7-step writing tool, now used by schools across the United States. It works by giving kids and teens the opportunity to write about their deepest personal difficulties, *Imagine* new possibilities, and amend their stories with brighter, more confident projections into the future.

Dianne is the author of the multi-award winning book *The Imagine Project: Stories of Courage, Hope and Love* (Yampa Valley Publishing, 2013). She also wrote *Byron the Caterpillar Who Loved to Imagine* (Yampa Valley Publishing, 2017) and *Your Premature Baby and Child (Berkley, 1999)*. She lives outside of Denver with her husband and has 3 grown children.

To find out more about Professional Development Trainings and Dianne's speaking engagements, go to www.theimagineproject.org or email Dianne at maroneyd@aol.com.

John Lennon showed us the power of the word Imagine when he asked us to Imagine Peace. In this inspirational and motivational book, the word Imagine is used to tell remarkable stories of ordinary people who have overcome and persevered through a variety of astonishing circumstances. The reader is invited to Imagine—to lose themselves if only for a short while—through reading these extraordinary stories of people from all across the US. Through listening to and reflecting on these incredible paths of personal fulfillment and transformation, you will feel encouraged, motivated, and inspired to turn inward and reflect on your own story.

The Imagine Project: Stories of Courage, Hope, and Love:
ISBN: 978-0-9889951-0-9, $35.00

Byron loves to Imagine! He imagines so much he can't stop talking about his dreams. When the animals in the forest tell him he will never be able to do the things he dreams of, Byron becomes very sad. Then he talks to the

wise old owl who tells him to go to a quiet place, write down his Imagine dreams, and listen to his heart. When he does magical things begin happening! *Byron the Caterpillar Who Loved to Imagine* teaches kids to believe in themselves, listen to their hearts, and ultimately follow their dreams. A wonderful book for kids age 10 and under!

Byron the Caterpillar Who Loved to Imagine!
ISBN: 978-0-9889951-7-8, Hard Cover,

For more information about *The Imagine Project, Inc.,*
go to www.theimagineproject.org

CPSIA information can be obtained
at www.ICGtesting.com
Printed in the USA
LVOW10s2334291117
558026LV00017B/1450/P